CHOCOLATE BASICS

MY COOKING CLASS

CHOCOLATE BASICS

80 RECIPES

ILLUSTRATED STEP BY STEP

ORATHAY GUILLAUMONT AND VANIA NIKOLCIC

PHOTOGRAPHS BY PIERRE JAVELLE

FIREFLY BOOKS

A FIREFLY BOOK

Published by Firefly Books Ltd. 2010

First printing

Publisher Cataloging-in-Publication Data (U.S.)
Guillaumont, Orathay.
Chocolate basics : 80 recipes illustrated step by step / Orathay Guillaumont and Vania Nikolcic; photographs by Pierre Javelle.
[256] p. : col. photos. ; cm.
Includes index.
ISBN-13: 978-1-55407-758-8 (pbk.)
ISBN-10: 1-55407-758-3 (pbk.)
1. Cookery (chocolate). I. Nikolcic, Vania. II. Javelle, Pierre. IV. Title.
641.6374 dc22 TX767.C5.G85 2010

Library and Archives Canada Cataloguing in Publication
Guillaumont, Orathay
Chocolate basics : 80 recipes illustrated step by step / Orathay Guillaumont and Vania Nikolcic.
Includes index.
ISBN-13: 978-1-55407-758-8 (pbk.)
ISBN-10: 1-55407-758-3 (pbk.)
1. Cookery (Chocolate). I. Nikolcic, Vania II. Title.
TX767.C5G85 2010 641.6'374 C2010-901587-8

Published in the United States by
Firefly Books (U.S.) Inc.
P.O. Box 1338, Ellicott Station
Buffalo, New York 14205

Published in Canada by
Firefly Books Ltd.
66 Leek Crescent
Richmond Hill, Ontario L4B 1H1

Printed in China

PREFACE

Chocolate . . . The abracadabra of fine foods.

This book, a veritable cocoa-fied book of spells, contains not only the classic incantations — rich chocolate cake, truffles or cookies — but also those destined to delight the most adventurous magicians, such as White Forest Cake and Matcha Marble Cake.

Black, white or praline magic. Creamy, foamy or crunchy. Here are 80 recipes that will delight every sense and bewitch the taste buds of young and old alike.

It is from this happy perspective that each recipe surrenders its secrets, step by step, inviting the amateur as well as the most experienced cooks to participate in each of the easy-to-follow preparations. You will see the chocolate melt heroically into the cream and spread its charms over an astounded genoise, only to greet with joy a sprinkling of coconut.

Image after image of sweet, simple treasures await you.

✻ ✻ ✻

CONTENTS

1

THE BASICS

2

RICH AND MOIST

3

FOAMY AND CREAMY

4

CRUNCHY AND SOFT

5

CAKES

6

CHIC AND PRECIOUS

7

PLAYFUL

APPENDIXES

THE BASICS

1

BUTTERCREAM

YIELD: 10½ OUNCES (300 G) • PREPARATION: 20 MINUTES • COOKING: 5 MINUTES

6 tablespoons (90 ml) superfine sugar
1¼ cups (310 ml) water
3 egg yolks, room temperature
⅔ cup (150 ml) butter, softened
1 vanilla bean, halved

VARIATION:
For chocolate-flavored buttercream, melt 2 ounces (60 g) dark chocolate and add along with the vanilla.

STORAGE:
Buttercream can be stored in a sealed container for 2 days in the refrigerator, or in the freezer. Before using, whisk for a few minutes.

1 2

3 4

1	Heat the sugar and water. Cook for about 5 minutes from the time the sugar has completely melted, to around 253°F (123°C).	2	Beat the egg yolks with an electric mixer until foamy and pale.
3	Incorporate the sugar into the yolks in a thin stream along the side of the bowl. Do not try to remove the sugar that sticks to the side, as this will create lumps. Next, beat at high speed to cool the mixture.	4	Reduce the speed of the mixer, gradually add the softened butter and then scrape the seeds from the vanilla bean and add them to the mixture. The buttercream is ready when the mixture is smooth and uniform.

2

CRÈME ANGLAISE

YIELD: 2 CUPS (500 ML) • PREPARATION: 15 MINUTES • COOKING: 10 MINUTES

2 cups (500 ml) milk
1 vanilla bean, halved and seeds scraped out
2½ tablespoons (37 ml) sugar
5 egg yolks
2 ounces (60 g) dark chocolate

VARIATION:
For vanilla crème anglaise, increase the amount of sugar to 6½ tablespoons (97 ml).

STORAGE:
It can be stored in the refrigerator for 2 days. Pour into a container, place plastic wrap directly on top of the cream to keep it from forming a crust and seal with a lid.

1	Bring the milk, the vanilla seeds and the scraped vanilla bean to a boil. Steep for 10 minutes. Remove the bean.	2	Whisk the sugar and egg yolks.	3	Pour half of the hot milk over the yolk mixture in a thin stream, stirring constantly.
4	Cook over low heat, stirring constantly, until the mixture thickens and coats a spoon.	5	Run your finger over the back of the spoon: if you can make a clean line, the cream is ready.	6	Remove from the heat, add the chocolate and stir until the chocolate is melted and the ingredients are combined.

3

PASTRY CREAM

→ YIELD: 1¾ POUNDS (800 G) • PREPARATION: 10 MINUTES • COOKING: 10 MINUTES ←

2 cups (500 ml) milk
4 egg yolks
½ cup (125 ml) sugar
2 tablespoons (30 ml) cornstarch
6 ounces (170 g) dark chocolate, chopped

VARIATION:
For vanilla pastry cream, omit the chocolate and steep a halved vanilla bean and its seeds in the milk.

STORAGE:
Follow the same method used for crème anglaise (see recipe 2).

1	Bring the milk to a boil.	2	Whisk the egg yolks with the sugar, then incorporate the cornstarch.	3	Pour half of the hot milk over the egg yolks, whisking constantly.
4	Place the mixture in a saucepan and cook over medium heat for 2 minutes, stirring constantly, until the cream thickens.	5	Remove from the heat and add the chocolate. Whisk until the mixture becomes a smooth cream.	6	Cool and use immediately or cover with plastic wrap (place it directly on top of the pastry cream) and refrigerate.

GENOISE

YIELD: 9-INCH (23 CM) ROUND OR SQUARE CAKE • PREPARATION: 25 MINUTES • BAKING: 25 MINUTES

¾ cup (175 ml) flour
¼ cup (60 ml) ground almonds
¼ cup (60 ml) cocoa powder
4 eggs
⅔ cup (150 ml) sugar

PRELIMINARY:
Preheat the oven to 350°F (180°C).
Butter and flour the baking pan.

1 2
3 4

1	Sift together the flour, ground almonds and cocoa. Set aside.	2	In a double boiler, beat the eggs and sugar with an electric mixer until the mixture thickens and triples in volume.
3	Once the mixture is warm, remove from the heat and continue to whip with a spatula until cool, about 10 minutes. The batter is ready when it forms a thick band.	4	Gradually add the flour mixture by carefully folding it into the batter, so as not to deflate it. ➤

4

5	Pour the batter into the pan and bake for 25 minutes.	**VARIATION** For a plain genoise, leave out the cocoa and add 1½ tablespoons (22 ml) cooled melted butter at the end.

4

6	Remove the genoise from the pan and allow to cool before cutting.	**STORAGE** When covered well with plastic wrap, the genoise can be kept for a day at room temperature. It can also be frozen.

SUGAR PASTRY

YIELD: 1 POUND (500 G) • PREPARATION: 15 MINUTES • RESTING: 1 HOUR

1¾ cups (375 ml) butter
½ cup (125 ml) sugar
1 egg
1⅔ cups (400 ml) flour
½ cup (125 ml) ground almonds
1 teaspoon (5 ml) vanilla extract

VARIATION:
For a chocolate-flavored pastry, add 1½ tablespoons (22 ml) cocoa powder to the flour.

STORAGE:
Wrapped well in plastic wrap, sugar pastry can be kept for 3 days in the refrigerator, and it can also be frozen.

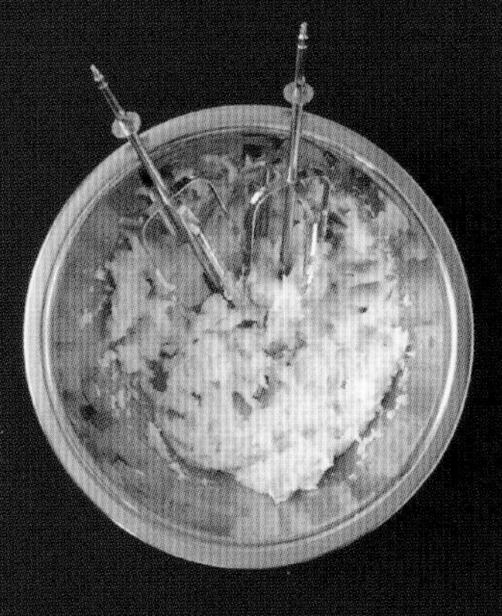

1 2

3 4

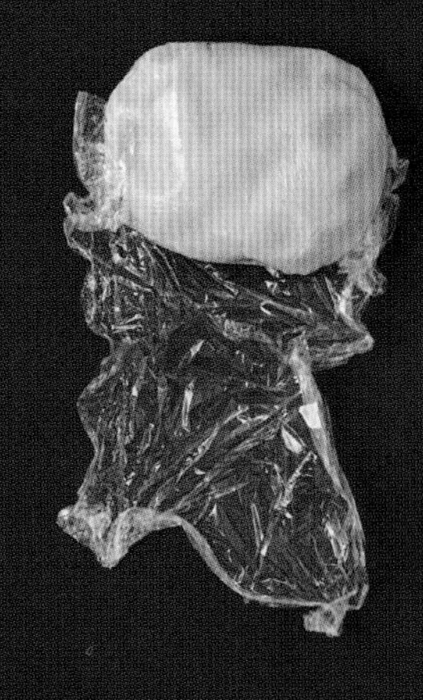

1	Using an electric mixer, beat the butter and sugar until creamy.	2	Add the egg and continue beating to combine.
3	Add the flour, ground almonds and vanilla extract. Ensure all of the ingredients are evenly combined, but do not overwork the pastry; at this stage, it should be soft and slightly sticky.	4	Transfer the pastry to plastic wrap and allow it to rest and harden in the refrigerator. The pastry is easier to roll out when cold.

6

EGG MOUSSE

YIELD: ABOUT 1 POUND (500 G) • PREPARATION: 15 MINUTES • COOKING: 5 MINUTES • RESTING: 2 HOURS

7 ounces (200 g) dark chocolate
7 tablespoons (105 ml) milk
2 egg yolks
4 egg whites

PRELIMINARY:
Chop the chocolate.

1

2

3

4

5

6

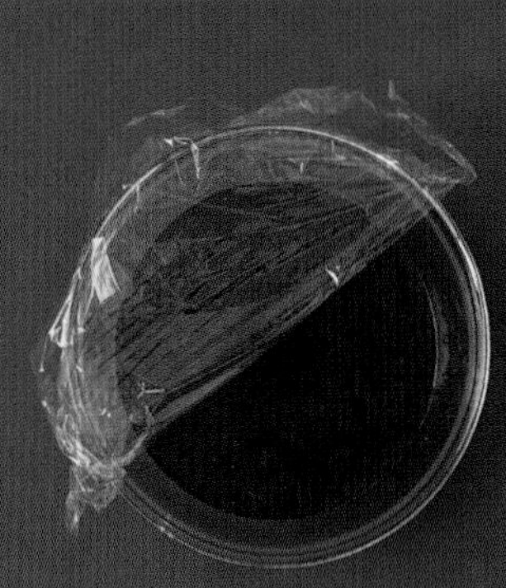

1	Bring the milk to a boil.	2	Pour the milk over the chocolate. Mix until the chocolate melts.	3	Add the egg yolks and whisk.
4	Whip the egg whites until stiff. Incorporate a third of the egg whites by whisking into the chocolate mixture.	5	Using a spatula, carefully fold the remaining egg whites into the chocolate mixture.	6	Set aside in the refrigerator for at least 2 hours to allow the mousse to set.

CREAM MOUSSE

YIELD: 14 OUNCES (400 G) • PREPARATION: 15 MINUTES • COOKING: 5 MINUTES

5 ounces (150 g) dark chocolate morsels (about ¾ cup/175 ml)
1 cup (250 ml) heavy cream (36%)

1 2

3 4

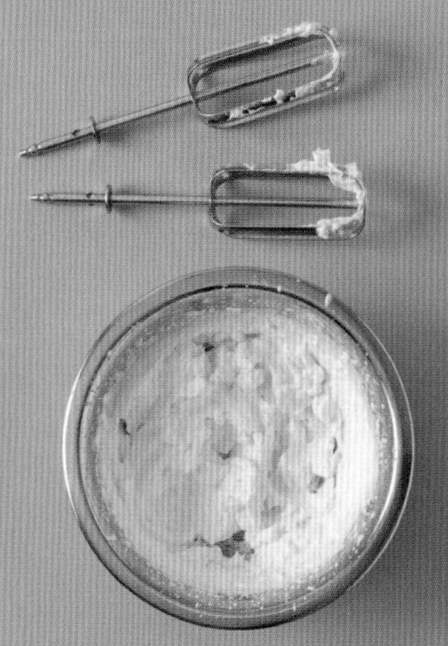

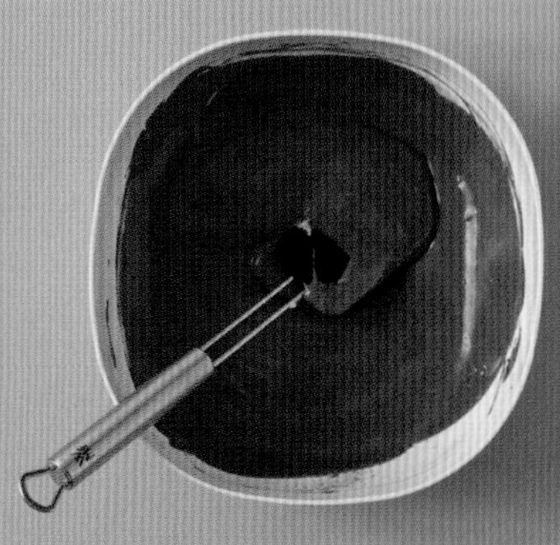

1	Bring ⅔ cup (150 ml) heavy cream to a boil, and then pour it over the chocolate morsels.	2	Wait 2 minutes, then whisk by stirring from the center and working your way out, until you have a smooth ganache. Leave to cool.
3	With an electric mixer, whip the remaining heavy cream until stiff.	4	Using a spatula, carefully fold the whipped cream into the chocolate mixture. Use immediately (see recipe 51 or 53).

CHOCOLATE GANACHE

YIELD: 10½ OUNCES (300 G) • PREPARATION: 10 MINUTES • COOKING: 5 MINUTES

⅔ cup (150 ml) heavy cream (36%)
5 ounces (150 g) chocolate, chopped

NOTE:
This ganache is easy to use and covers cakes well. Sealed in plastic wrap, it can be stored in the refrigerator for several days.

Heat on low in a microwave oven to reuse it in a chocolate pie, in truffles or as icing on an 8- or 9-inch (20 or 23 cm) diameter cake.

1 2
3 4

1	Bring the cream to a boil.	2	Pour the cream over the chopped chocolate.
3	Wait 2 minutes, then mix by whisking in a circular motion, starting in the center and working your way out.	4	The ganache is ready when the mixture is smooth, shiny and uniform.

9

FANCY ICING

YIELD: COVERS ONE 8- OR 9-INCH (20 OR 23 CM) DIAMETER CAKE
PREPARATION: 15 MINUTES • RESTING: 30 MINUTES

½ cup (125 ml) sugar
3 tablespoons (45 ml) milk powder
3½ tablespoons (52 ml) cocoa powder
7 tablespoons (105 ml) heavy cream (36%)
⅛ ounce (3.5 g) unflavored gelatin powder, or 2 sheets gelatin

NOTE:
This icing can be prepared several days in advance. Store in the refrigerator and carefully reheat in a double boiler or microwave oven when ready to use.

1 2

3 4

1	Bring all the ingredients, except the gelatin, to a boil.	2	Cook over low heat for 15 minutes, stirring occasionally.
3	Dissolve the gelatin in a little cold water (if using sheet gelatin, soak in cold water until softened, then drain). Incorporate the prepared gelatin into the chocolate mixture.	4	Mix well and set aside for 30 minutes before using; this gives the icing time to set, and it will cover the cake better.

10

HAZELNUT PRALINE PASTE

YIELD: ABOUT 1 POUND (500 G) • PREPARATION: 20 MINUTES • COOKING: 10 MINUTES • RESTING: 30 MINUTES

1⅓ cups (325 ml) sugar
1 vanilla bean
9 ounces (250 g) whole hazelnuts

VARIATION:
To prepare a traditional praline paste, substitute almonds for half of the hazelnuts (use the same amount of sugar).

STORAGE:
Praline paste can be stored in a sealed jar in the refrigerator for several weeks.

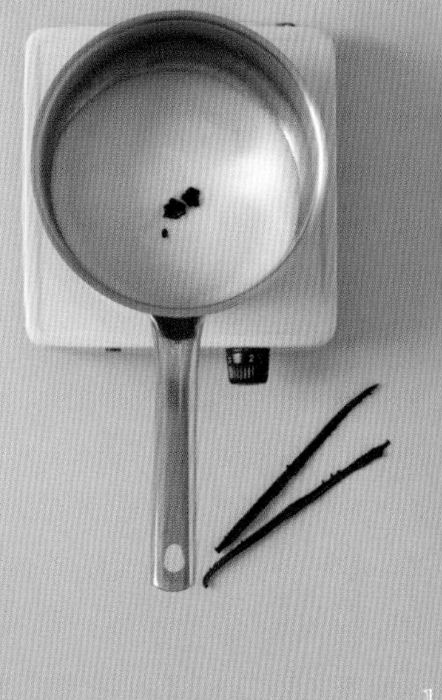

1 2 3

4 5 6

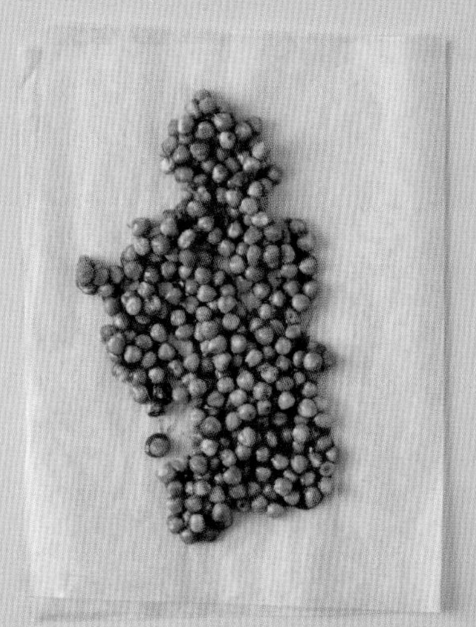

1	Over low heat, melt the sugar and the seeds from the vanilla bean; do not stir.	2	Cook until the sugar caramelizes.	3	Remove from the heat and then add the whole hazelnuts. Mix to completely coat.
4	Pour the caramelized hazelnuts onto parchment paper. Leave to cool.	5	Once they have cooled, blend the hazelnuts in a food processor until smooth.	6	It’s ready!

11

CHOCOLATE-HAZELNUT SPREAD

YIELD: 14 OUNCES (400 G) • PREPARATION: 10 MINUTES • COOKING: 5 MINUTES

7 ounces (200 g) hazelnut-flavored milk chocolate
½ ounce (15 g) dark chocolate
½ cup (125 ml) sweetened condensed milk
¼ cup (60 ml) heavy cream (36%)

VARIATION:
Substitute 4 ounces (120 g) praline paste (see recipe 10) and 3 ounces (80 g) milk chocolate for the hazelnut-flavored milk chocolate.

1 2
3 4

1	Place all the ingredients in a double boiler.	2	Heat, whisking constantly.
3	Stir until all of the chocolate is melted and the mixture is uniform.	4	Pour into a jar.

12

CHOCOLATE DECORATIONS

YIELD: 7 OUNCES (200 G) • PREPARATION: 10 TO 20 MINUTES • COOKING: 10 MINUTES

7 ounces (200 g) white chocolate morsels (about 1 cup/250 ml)
7 ounces (200 g) milk chocolate
7 ounces (200 g) dark chocolate morsels (about 1 cup/250 ml)

1 2 3

4 5 6

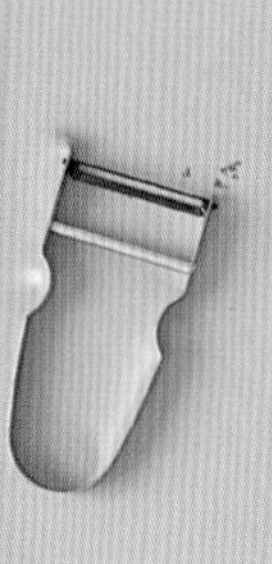

1	Prepare the chocolate morsels separately by melting ⅔ in a double boiler and then adding the remaining third and mixing well.	2	To make dark chocolate curls, pour the melted chocolate onto a smooth surface and spread out evenly with a spatula. Cool at room temperature.	3	Hold a knife at a 45° angle and push it away from yourself with a sudden, sharp movement.
4	To make milk chocolate shavings, use a vegetable peeler to scrape the side of a solid bar of chocolate.	5	To make shapes, use a spoon to draw with melted white chocolate on a sheet of waxed paper.	6	The decorations can be stored in a container in the refrigerator.

RICH AND MOIST

2

CHOCOLATE LOAF

YIELD: 6 SERVINGS • PREPARATION: 20 MINUTES • BAKING: 40 MINUTES

8½ ounces (240 g) dark chocolate
7 tablespoons (105 ml) butter
6 eggs

1⅔ cups (400 ml) ground almonds
6½ tablespoons (97 ml) sugar

PRELIMINARY:
Preheat the oven to 340 °F (170 °C).
Roughly chop 3½ ounces (100 g) chocolate.

1	Melt 5 ounces (140 g) chocolate and the butter in a microwave oven or double boiler.	2	Separate the egg whites from the yolks.	3	Add the egg yolks to the chocolate, mix and then mix in the ground almonds.
4	With an electric mixer, whip the egg whites until stiff, gradually adding the sugar as you work.	5	Fold the stiff egg whites and chocolate pieces into the chocolate-almond mixture.	6	Pour into a buttered and floured 9- x 5-inch (23 x 13 cm) long pan. Bake for 35 to 40 minutes.

14

MATCHA MARBLE CAKE

YIELD: 6 SERVINGS • PREPARATION: 30 MINUTES • BAKING: 50 MINUTES

1⅔ cups (400 ml) flour
1 tablespoon (15 ml) baking powder
⅓ cup (75 ml) milk
2 tablespoons (30 ml) cocoa powder
1 to 1½ tablespoons (15 to 22 ml) matcha
¾ cup (175 ml) butter, softened
1⅞ cups (460 ml) confectioners' sugar
4 eggs
¾ cup (175 ml) ground almonds

PRELIMINARY:
Preheat the oven to 350°F (180°C).
Sift together the flour and baking powder.

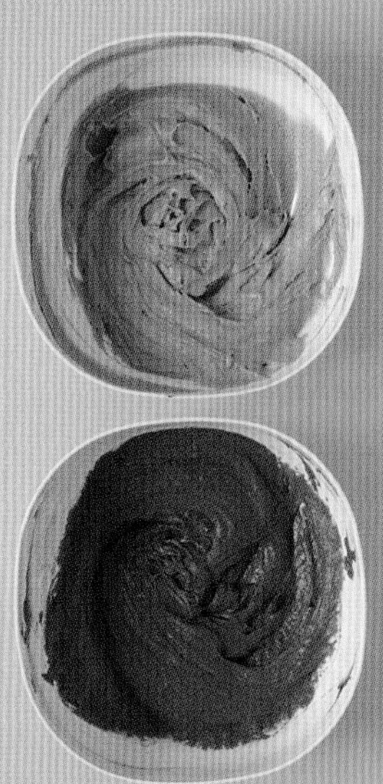

1	Warm the milk in a microwave oven. In a small bowl, dilute the cocoa with half of the milk, and, in another container, mix the remaining milk with the matcha. Set aside.	2	Whip the softened butter with the confectioners' sugar.	
3	Add the eggs one by one, then mix in the flour and ground almonds.	4	Divide the batter in half. Add the cocoa mixture to one half of the batter and the matcha mixture to the other half.	➢

5	Alternately pour the different batters to layer in a buttered and floured 9-inch (23 cm) loaf pan.	**TIP** ☛ To create the marble pattern, pour half of the chocolate batter, cover with the matcha batter and then finish with the remaining chocolate batter. Next, run a knife along the entire length, raising it from time to time.

6	Bake for 45 to 50 minutes.

15

CUPCAKES

YIELD: 10 TO 12 CUPCAKES • PREPARATION: 40 MINUTES • BAKING: 20 MINUTES

⅔ cup (150 ml) butter
3 tablespoons (45 ml) cocoa powder
1⅓ cups (325 ml) self-rising flour
½ cup (125 ml) yogurt
3 eggs
⅔ cup (150 ml) brown sugar
1 teaspoon (5 ml) vanilla extract

FOR THE ITALIAN MERINGUE:
1⅔ cups (400 ml) sugar
⅓ cup (75 ml) water
2 egg whites

PRELIMINARY:
Preheat the oven to 375°F (190°C). Melt the butter. Sift together the cocoa and flour.

1 2
3 4

1	In a large bowl, whisk the yogurt, eggs, brown sugar and vanilla extract.	2	Add the flour and cocoa. Whisk without overworking the batter, then add the melted butter.
3	Line a muffin pan or molds with paper liners. Pour batter into each liner and smooth the surface.	4	Bake for 20 minutes, rotating the pan halfway through so the cupcakes cook evenly. Allow to cool before icing. ➢

15

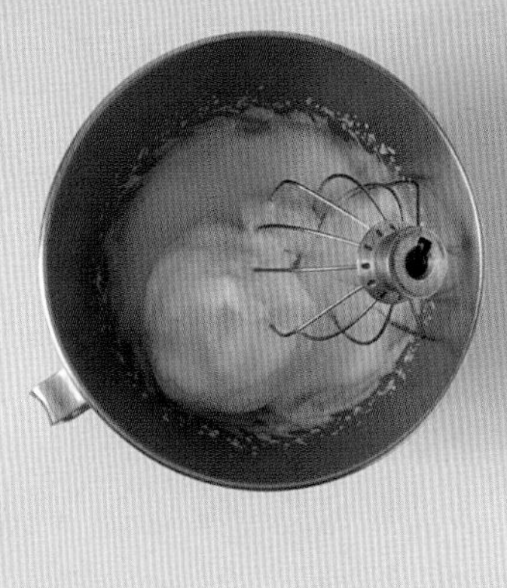

5 6
7 8

5	To make the meringue, bring the sugar and water to a boil, then cook for 5 minutes, without stirring.	6	With an electric mixer, whisk the egg whites until stiff.
7	Reduce the speed and pour the sugar syrup into the egg whites in a thin stream. Whip for 10 minutes, until the mixture is firm and cold.	8	Using a pastry bag, decorate the cupcakes with the meringue.

9	Dust the cupcakes with sugar sprinkles.	**TIP** ☛ You can also ice the cupcakes with a spoon, using the back to form little peaks in the meringue.

WHIPPED CHOCOLATE FROSTING

CUPCAKE VARIATION

Prepare 10 to 12 cupcakes (see recipe 15). Prepare a batch of chocolate whipped cream (see recipe 27) using 3½ ounces (100 g) chocolate and 1 cup (250 ml) heavy cream (36%). Melt the chocolate with 3½ tablespoons (52 ml) of the cream. Mix, then add the remaining cream, which must be very cold. Carefully whip the cream in a bowl sitting in an ice bath. Ice the cupcakes using a pastry bag.

WHIPPED VANILLA FROSTING

CUPCAKE VARIATION

Prepare 10 to 12 cupcakes (see recipe 15). Prepare a batch of vanilla whipped cream using ⅞ cup (200 ml) heavy cream (36%), the seeds scraped from 1 vanilla bean and 2 tablespoons (30 ml) confectioners' sugar.

Whip the cream along with the vanilla seeds, gradually adding the confectioners' sugar. Ice the cupcakes using a spatula.

CHOCOLATE & COCONUT SQUARES

YIELD: 24 SQUARES • PREPARATION: 20 MINUTES • BAKING: 25 MINUTES • RESTING: 10 MINUTES

FOR THE GENOISE:

4 eggs
1 cup (250 ml) flour
⅔ cup (150 ml) sugar
1½ tablespoons (22 ml) butter, melted and cooled

FOR THE COATING:

7 ounces (200 g) dark chocolate
⅞ cup (200 ml) heavy cream (36%)
1½ tablespoons (22 ml) butter
2½ cups (625 ml) shredded coconut

1 2

3 4

1	Prepare a batch of genoise batter (see recipe 4). Pour onto a small rimmed baking sheet and bake at 350°F (180°C) for 25 minutes. Cut into 1½-inch (4 cm) squares.	2	Prepare a ganache (see recipe 8) using the chocolate and cream, and then add the butter. The coating is ready once it is smooth and shiny.
3	Pour the coconut onto a plate. Using 2 wooden skewers or 2 forks, dip each square into the chocolate, then roll in the coconut.	4	Chill for 10 minutes in the refrigerator before serving.

CHOCOLATE MADELEINES

YIELD: ABOUT 15 MADELEINES • PREPARATION: 15 MINUTES • RESTING: OVERNIGHT • BAKING: 10 MINUTES

⅔ cup (150 ml) flour
1½ teaspoons (7 ml) baking powder
3 tablespoons (45 ml) cocoa powder
7 tablespoons (105 ml) butter, softened

6½ tablespoons (97 ml) superfine sugar
2 tablespoons (30 ml) honey
1 teaspoon (5 ml) vanilla extract
2 eggs

PRELIMINARY:
Preheat the oven to 425°F (220°C).
Sift together the flour, baking powder and cocoa.

1 2

3 4

1	Whisk the softened butter with the sugar, honey and vanilla.	2	Add the eggs one by one, whisking to combine. Next add the flour mixture. Place in the refrigerator for 2 hours or overnight, if possible.
3	Fill the madeleine cups three-quarters full and bake in a 425°F (220°C) oven for 5 minutes.	4	Lower the temperature to 350°F (180°C) and continue baking for another 5 minutes. Turn the madeleines out of the pan and eat immediately.

RICH CHOCOLATE CAKE

→ **YIELD: 8 SERVINGS** • PREPARATION: 20 MINUTES • BAKING: 25 MINUTES ←

7 ounces (200 g) chocolate
⅞ cup (210 ml) butter
¾ cup (175 ml) sugar
5 eggs
1 tablespoon (15 ml) flour

PRELIMINARY:
Preheat the oven to 350°F (180°C).

1 2
3 4

1	Melt the chocolate and butter in a double boiler or microwave oven.	2	Add the sugar and whisk. Set aside.	
3	Separate the egg whites from the yolks.	4	Whisk the egg whites with an electric mixer until stiff (but not too stiff, so they will be easier to combine with the chocolate mixture).	➢

5 6
7 8

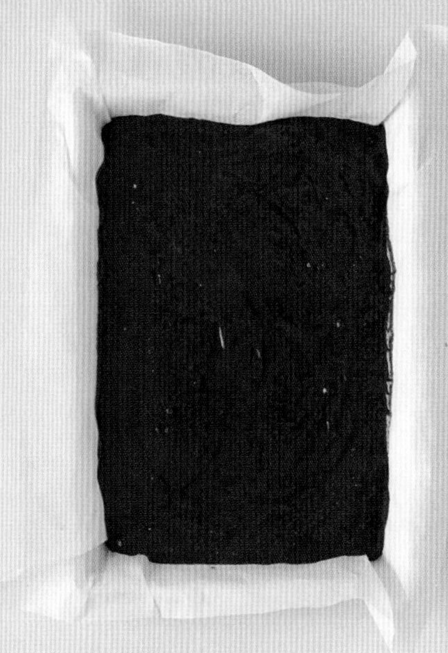

5	Once the chocolate mixture has cooled, mix in the egg yolks.	6	Add the sifted flour and mix.
7	Next, gradually fold in the beaten egg whites. Start with 2 spoonfuls, fold until the mixture is uniform and then add the rest of the whites.	8	Line a baking pan with parchment paper, pour in the mixture and bake for 20 to 25 minutes.

9	It's ready! Eat warm or cold.	**TIP** ☛ To check doneness, insert a knife into the middle of the cake. The blade should come out moist but not sticky. **VARIATION** Substitute 1 cup (250 ml) ground almonds for the flour.

MINI MOLTEN CHOCOLATE CAKES

YIELD: 4 SERVINGS • PREPARATION: 15 MINUTES • BAKING: 7 MINUTES

7 ounces (200 g) dark chocolate
⅓ cup (75 ml) butter
4 eggs
⅓ cup (75 ml) sugar
⅓ cup + 1 tablespoon (90 ml) flour, sifted

PRELIMINARY:
Preheat the oven to 425°F (220°C).

1 2
3 4

1	Melt the chocolate and butter together in a double boiler or microwave oven. Set aside.	2	Whisk the eggs and sugar until the mixture is pale and foamy.
3	Add the egg mixture to the cooled chocolate mixture. Stir, then mix in the flour. Add a little extra flour if the batter doesn't come together.	4	Pour the batter into buttered and floured ramekins or a buttered and floured muffin pan. Bake for 7 minutes, allow to rest for 2 minutes and then remove from the ramekins.

MINI MOLTEN CARAMEL CAKES

VARIATION OF MOLTEN CHOCOLATE CAKES

Prepare the chocolate batter (see recipe 21). Fill 4 ramekins halfway with the batter.

Place a caramel candy in the center, then cover with batter. Bake for 9 minutes.

MINI MOLTEN VANILLA CAKES

VARIATION OF MOLTEN CHOCOLATE CAKES

Prepare the chocolate batter (see recipe 21). Fill 4 ramekins halfway with the batter.

Place a small scoop of vanilla ice cream in the center, then cover with batter. Bake for 9 minutes.

MUFFINS

YIELD: 6 MUFFINS • PREPARATION: 20 MINUTES • BAKING: 30 MINUTES

2½ tablespoons (37 ml) flour
½ teaspoon (2 ml) yeast
4½ ounces (135 g) dark chocolate morsels (about ⅔ cup/150 ml)
2½ tablespoons (37 ml) oil
3 eggs
¼ cup (60 ml) sugar
2½ tablespoons (37 ml) honey
1⅓ cup (325 ml) ground almonds

PRELIMINARY:
Sift the flour and yeast together. Preheat the oven to 325°F (160°C).

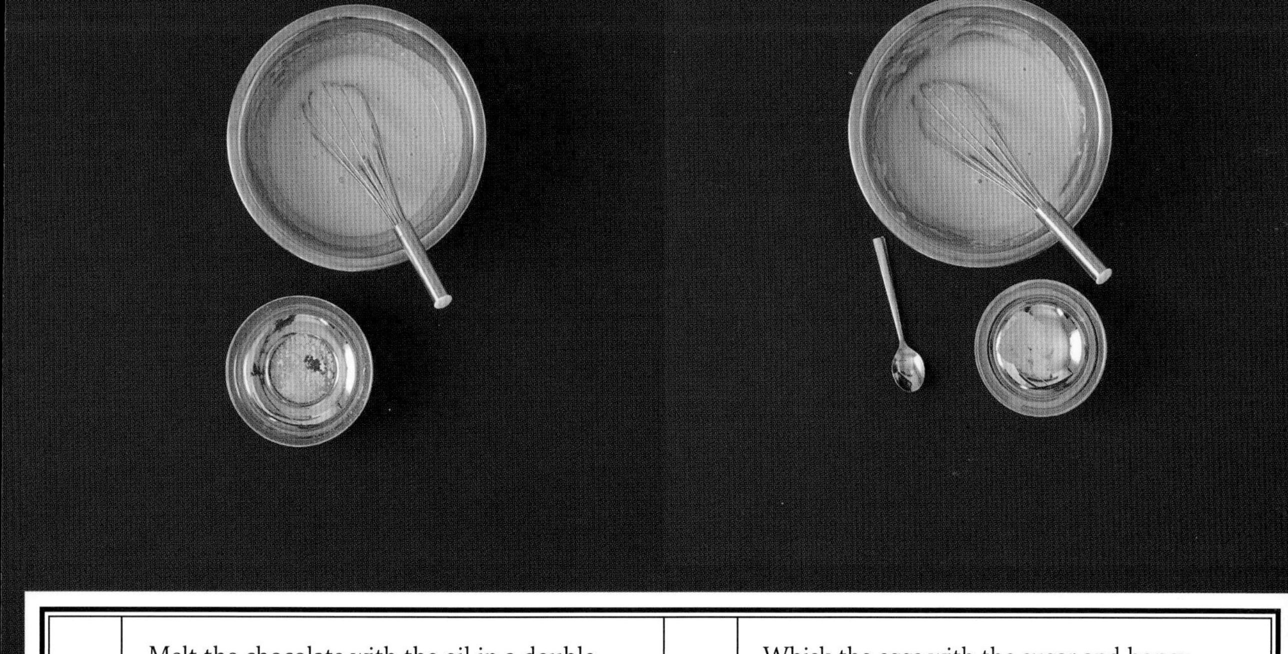

1	Melt the chocolate with the oil in a double boiler or microwave oven. Set aside.	2	Whisk the eggs with the sugar and honey.	
3	Whisk in the ground almonds.	4	Gradually sprinkle the flour and yeast into the egg mixture and whisk in.	➢

5	Fold the egg mixture into the chocolate mixture with a spatula.	**VARIATION** Add chunks of milk, white or dark chocolate to the batter.

6	Fill the muffin cups, then bake for about 30 minutes.	**TIP** ☛ Insert a toothpick into the center of each muffin to check doneness. If the toothpick comes out clean, the muffins are done.

FOAMY AND CREAMY

3

EASY CHOCOLATE MOUSSE

YIELD: 6 SERVINGS • PREPARATION: 15 MINUTES • RESTING: 3 HOURS

6 eggs
7 ounces (200 g) dark chocolate

PRELIMINARY:
Separate the egg whites from the yolks.

1 2
3 4

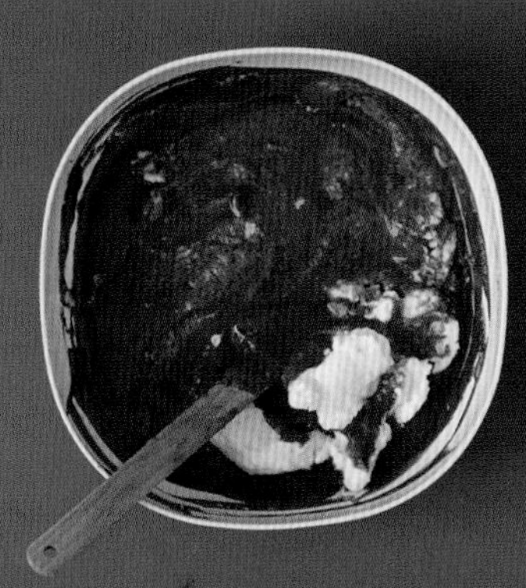

1	Melt the chocolate in a double boiler or microwave oven, add the egg yolks and mix. Set aside to cool.	2	With an electric mixer, whisk the egg whites until stiff (but not too stiff, so they can be easily incorporated into the chocolate).
3	Once the chocolate is cooled but still warm, carefully fold in the whites.	4	Refrigerate for at least 3 hours.

SPICED HOT CHOCOLATE

YIELD: 6 SERVINGS • PREPARATION: 20 MINUTES

2 cups (500 ml) milk
1 cup (250 ml) heavy cream (36%)
2 vanilla beans
1 small stick cinnamon
1 section of star anise
1 clove

5 ounces (150 g) chocolate (at least 60% cocoa)
1¾ ounces (50 g) milk chocolate morsels (about ¼ cup/60 ml)

TIP: This hot chocolate is better if prepared the day before, stored in the refrigerator and strained at the last moment. Carefully reheat in a saucepan or microwave oven. It is also delicious served cold.

26

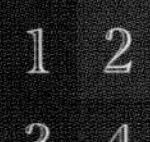

1	In a saucepan, warm the milk and cream with the seeds from the vanilla beans, the scraped beans, the cinnamon, the star anise and the clove.	2	Remove from the heat and allow to steep for 10 minutes.
3	Next, bring the mixture to a boil, remove from the heat and then add the chocolate and morsels. Mix, then strain.	4	Blend briefly in a blender or whisk by hand to make the hot chocolate foamy and serve.

UPSIDE-DOWN CHOCOLATE SUNDAE

→ YIELD: 4 SERVINGS • PREPARATION: 30 MINUTES • BAKING: 10 MINUTES ←

FOR THE CHOCOLATE WHIPPED CREAM:

⅔ cup (150 ml) heavy cream (36%), very cold
1 heaping teaspoon (5 ml) honey
1¾ ounces (50 g) dark chocolate, chopped

FOR THE CHOCOLATE SAUCE:

3½ ounces (100 g) dark chocolate
⅞ cup (200 ml) water
⅔ cup (150 ml) crème fraîche or sour cream
Seeds from 1 vanilla bean

2 cups (500 ml) vanilla ice cream
4 small meringues, coarsely broken

1	Carefully cook all the sauce ingredients for 10 minutes.	2	Bring ¼ cup (60 ml) heavy cream and the honey to a boil.	3	Pour the cream mixture into the chocolate. Whisk, then add 7 tablespoons (105 ml) of very cold cream.
4	Plunge the chocolate mixture into an ice bath.	5	Carefully whip the chocolate cream with an electric mixer until semi-stiff.	6	In glasses, layer the ice cream, meringue pieces and whipped cream. Top with sauce and finish with a whipped cream rosette.

CHOCOLATE MILKSHAKE

YIELD: 2 LARGE SERVINGS • PREPARATION: 15 MINUTES

1⅔ cups (400 ml) milk
1½ tablespoons (22 ml) superfine sugar
2 tablespoons (30 ml) cocoa powder
2½ ounces (75 g) dark chocolate
1 vanilla bean, seeds scraped out
1 ounce (20 g) dark chocolate, shaved
⅞ cup (200 ml) heavy cream (36%)
1 tablespoon (15 ml) confectioners' sugar
8 to 10 ice cubes

TIP:
For foodies, add 1 tablespoon (15 ml) chocolate-hazelnut spread (see recipe 11) before blending with the ice cubes.

1 2
3 4

1	Bring the milk, sugar, cocoa, vanilla seeds and scraped vanilla bean to a boil. Remove from the heat, remove the vanilla bean and add the chocolate. Stir.	2	Using an electric mixer, whip the cream with the icing sugar. Set aside in the refrigerator.
3	Pour the cold chocolate into a blender, add the ice cubes and blend.	4	Transfer into 2 large glasses, divide up the whipped cream and sprinkle with chocolate shavings. Drink immediately.

CHOCOLATE TRIO

→ YIELD: 8 SERVINGS • PREPARATION: 30 MINUTES • RESTING: 3½ HOURS ←

FOR THE CRUST:
4½ ounces (125 g) chocolate wafer cookies
6½ ounces (180 g) hazelnut-flavored milk chocolate

FOR THE MOUSSES:
⅔ cup (150 ml) heavy cream (36%)
5 ounces (150 g) dark chocolate
⅔ cup (150 ml) milk
5 ounces (150 g) milk chocolate
5 ounces (150 g) white chocolate

PRELIMINARY:
Crush the wafers between your fingers.

1 2

3 4

1	Melt the hazelnut-flavored milk chocolate in a microwave oven or double boiler.	2	Pour the chocolate over the wafers and mix well to ensure all the pieces are coated.	
3	Pour the wafer mixture into a springform pan. Spread evenly and tamp down using a spoon to form a crust. Allow to set in a cool place for 30 minutes.	4	Whip the cream until stiff.	➢

5 6

7 8

5	Melt the dark chocolate with a third of the milk in a microwave oven or double boiler.	6	Fold a third of the whipped cream into the warm chocolate and pour over the crust. Allow to set for 45 minutes in the freezer.
7	Repeat steps 5 and 6 with the milk chocolate.	8	Repeat steps 5 and 6 for the white chocolate. If the whipped cream has begun to sink, whip slightly.

9	Before turning the cake out of the pan, let thaw for 1 hour in the refrigerator.	**VARIATION** Substitute 3 ounces (80 g) melted milk chocolate combined with 4 ounces (120 g) praline paste (see recipe 10) for the hazelnut-flavored milk chocolate.

CHOCOLATE PASSION IN A GLASS

YIELD: 4 SERVINGS • PREPARATION: 20 MINUTES • RESTING: 2 HOURS

FOR THE PASSION FRUIT CREAM:
8 passion fruits
2 egg yolks
1 tablespoon (15 ml) sugar
1 ounce (25 g) butter, softened

FOR THE CHOCOLATE MOUSSE:
⅔ cup (150 ml) heavy cream (36%)
3 ounces (80 g) milk chocolate morsels (about 7 tbsp/105 ml)

PRELIMINARY:
Strain the seeds from 6 passion fruits, to separate the pulp, and set the pulp aside. Remove the seeds, and pulp, from the 2 remaining fruits and set aside.

☛ To prepare 8 servings, use 2 egg yolks and 1 whole egg.

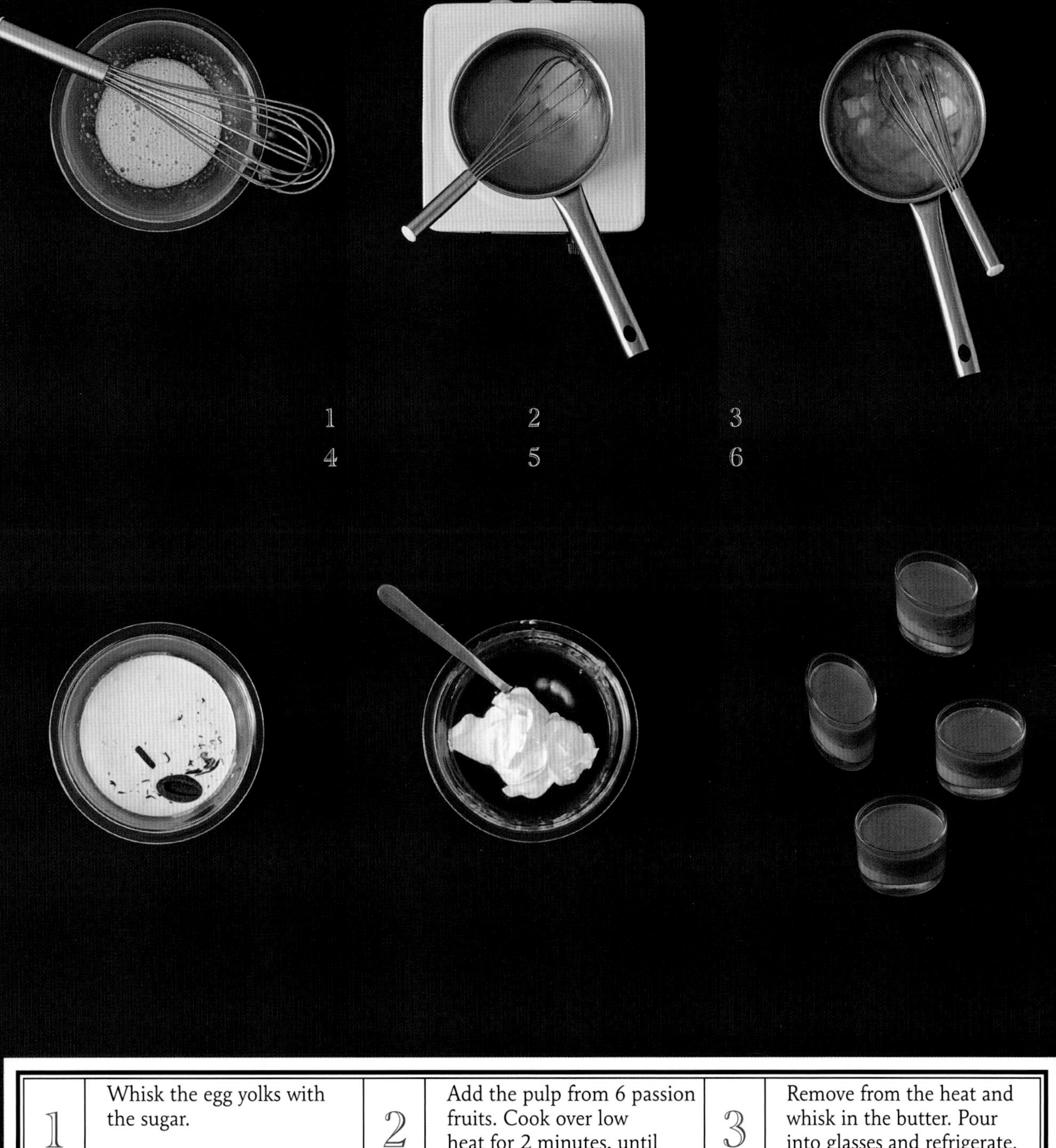

1	Whisk the egg yolks with the sugar.	2	Add the pulp from 6 passion fruits. Cook over low heat for 2 minutes, until thickened.	3	Remove from the heat and whisk in the butter. Pour into glasses and refrigerate.
4	Bring about 7 tablespoons (100 ml) cream to a boil. Pour over the pieces of chocolate and mix. Allow to cool.	5	Whip about ¼ cup (50 ml) cream and carefully fold into the warm chocolate mixture.	6	Distribute the passion fruit seeds among the glasses and layer the chocolate mousse on top. Allow to set in the refrigerator for 2 hours.

CREAM PUFFS

YIELD: 40 PUFFS • PREPARATION: 1 HOUR • BAKING: 25 MINUTES • RESTING: 40 MINUTES

FOR THE PASTRY CREAM:
2 cups (500 ml) milk
4 egg yolks
½ cup (125 ml) sugar
2 tablespoons (30 ml) cornstarch
6 ounces (170 g) dark chocolate, coarsely chopped

FOR THE CHOUX PASTRY:
½ cup (125 ml) milk
½ cup (125 ml) water
7½ tablespoons (112 ml) butter
½ teaspoon (2 ml) salt
½ tablespoon (7 ml) sugar
1 cup + 1 tablespoon (265 ml) flour, sifted
4 eggs

FOR THE GANACHE:
⅔ cup (150 ml) heavy cream (36%)
5 ounces (150 g) chocolate

PRELIMINARY:
Preheat the oven to 500°F (260°C). Bring the milk for the pastry cream to a boil.

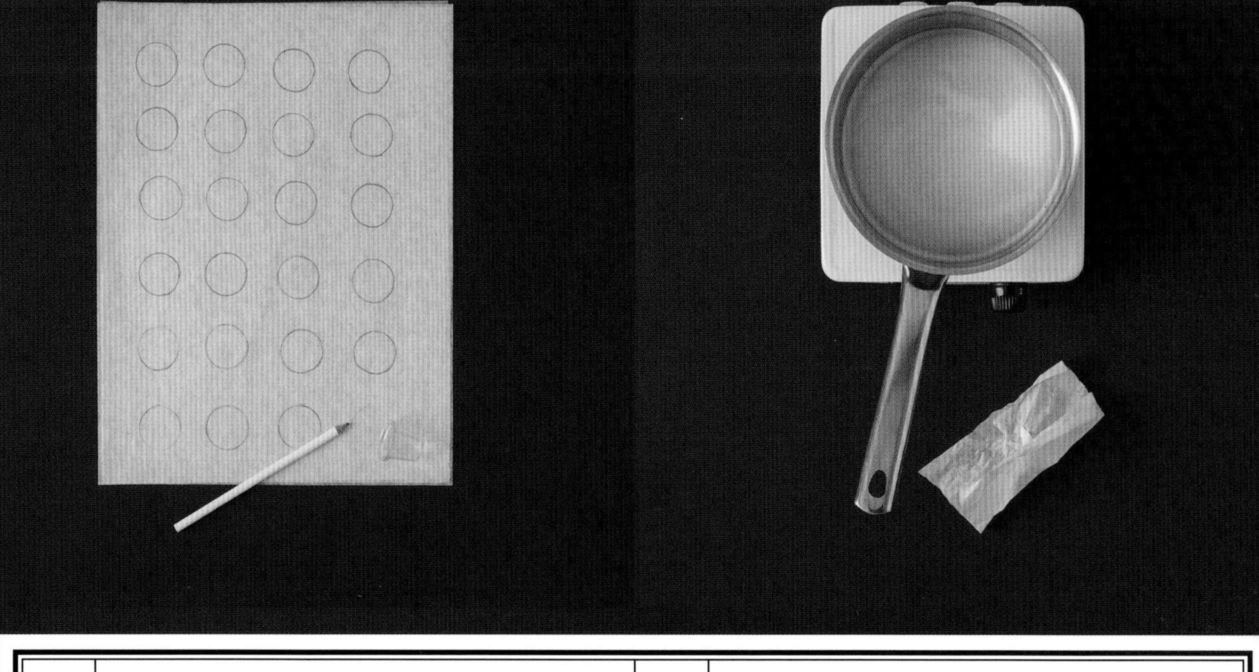

1	Prepare the pastry cream (see recipe 3) by pouring the hot milk over the egg yolk mixture, then cook for 2 minutes, stirring constantly.	2	Remove from the heat and add the chocolate. Whisk until smooth. Allow to cool, then cover the cream with plastic wrap.	
3	On parchment paper, draw 1½-inch (4 cm) diameter circles. Turn the paper over onto a baking sheet. Set aside.	4	Bring the milk, water, butter, salt and sugar for the choux pastry to a boil.	➢

5	Remove from the heat and add all the flour at once. Mix.	6	Place over the heat and stir until the pastry no longer sticks to the sides of the pan and forms a ball, about 2 minutes.
7	Remove from the heat and let the pastry cool slightly. Gradually add the 4 eggs one at a time, mixing quickly.	8	Fill a pastry bag with choux pastry and pipe small balls on the circles on the parchment paper.

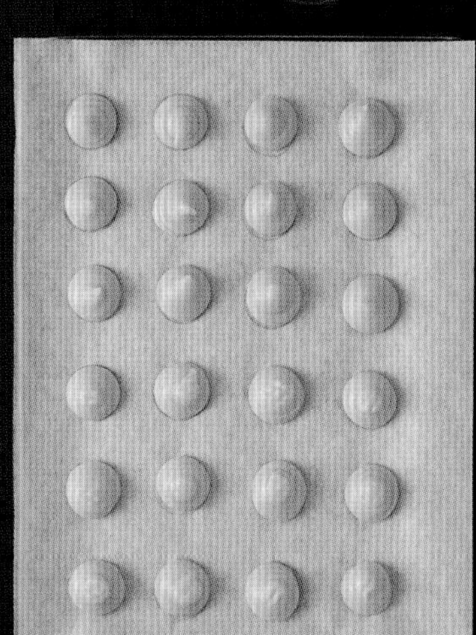

9 10

11 12

9	Dip a fork in cold water and lightly tap each ball to give it a more regular shape.	10	Lower the oven temperature to 325°F (160°C) and bake for 20 to 25 minutes. Allow to cool on a rack.
11	Pierce the bottom of the puffs with the pastry bag's tip.	12	Fill a pastry bag with pastry cream and fill the puffs. Set aside in the refrigerator. ➢

13	Prepare the ganache (see recipe 8) using the heavy cream and chocolate. Dip each puff in the ganache. Place on a baking sheet, then set aside in a cool location.	**TIP** ☛ To coat the puffs, dip them in the ganache, then wipe any drips with your index finger.

14

Once the icing has hardened, eat immediately.

VARIATIONS

The puffs can also be filled with chocolate–praline paste cream (see recipe 10) or egg mousse (see recipe 6).

CHOCOLATE MARQUISE

YIELD: 8 SERVINGS • PREPARATION: 20 MINUTES • RESTING: OVERNIGHT

7 ounces (200 g) dark chocolate
3 eggs
7 tablespoons (105 ml) butter, softened
2 egg whites

PRELIMINARY:
Melt the chocolate in a microwave oven or double boiler. Separate the 3 eggs.

1	Add the 3 egg yolks to the melted chocolate. Whisk.	2	Using a spatula, work the softened butter until creamy.	3	Add the butter to the chocolate mixture.
4	With an electric mixer, whisk the 5 egg whites until stiff.	5	Whisk ⅓ of the egg whites into the chocolate mixture. Once the mixture is smooth, carefully fold in the rest of the egg whites using a spatula.	6	Pour into a silicone loaf pan. Store in the refrigerator overnight, then slice to serve.

WHITE CHOCOLATE PANNA COTTA

YIELD: 4 SERVINGS • PREPARATION: 15 MINUTES • RESTING: 2 HOURS

½ ounce (14 g) unflavored gelatin powder
1¼ cup (310 ml) milk
7 tablespoons (105 ml) heavy cream (36%)
3 ounces (90 g) white chocolate
or 8 sheets gelatin

FOR THE RASPBERRY COULIS:
5 ounces (150 g) frozen raspberries
1½ tablespoons (22 ml) sugar
1 lime

PRELIMINARY:
Dissolve the gelatin in a little cold water (if using gelatin sheets, soak in cold water).

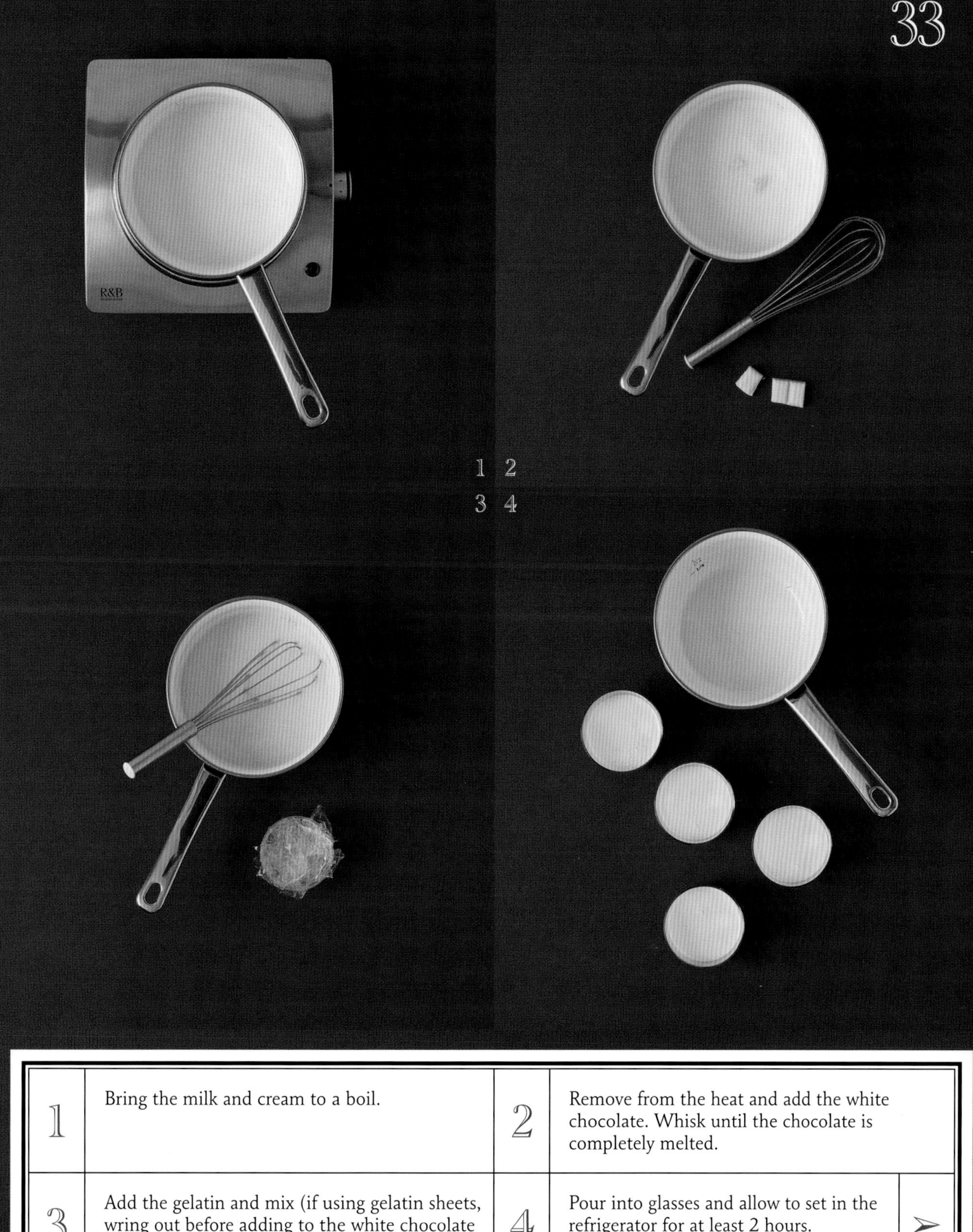

1	Bring the milk and cream to a boil.	2	Remove from the heat and add the white chocolate. Whisk until the chocolate is completely melted.	
3	Add the gelatin and mix (if using gelatin sheets, wring out before adding to the white chocolate mixture).	4	Pour into glasses and allow to set in the refrigerator for at least 2 hours.	➢

5

Cook the raspberries and sugar. Once the mixture is well stewed, strain to remove any seeds. Add lime zest and 1 tablespoon (15 ml) lime juice.

6	Once the panna cotta is set, pour the raspberry coulis on top and set aside in the refrigerator until ready to serve.

COULIS VARIATIONS

Use frozen coulis or Sachertorte apricot compote (see recipe 56) instead.

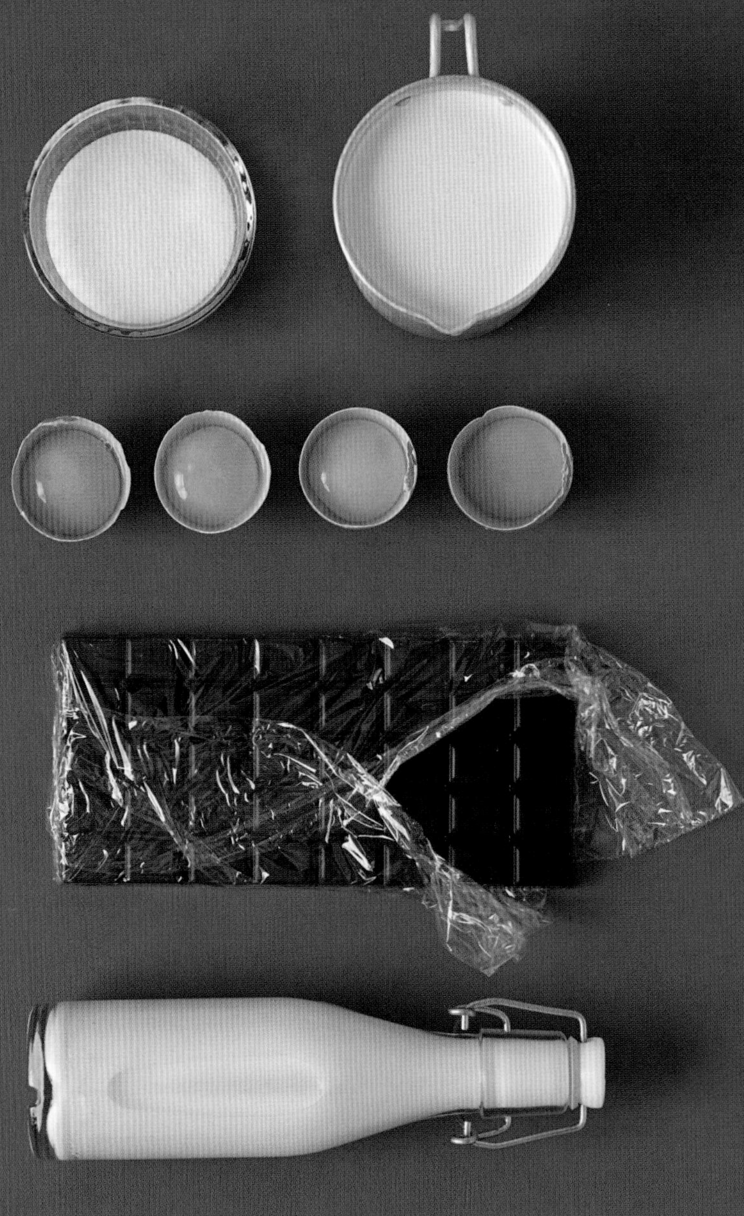

MINI POTS DE CRÈME

YIELD: 6 SERVINGS • PREPARATION: 15 MINUTES • RESTING: 3 HOURS

7 ounces (200 g) dark chocolate
1 cup (250 ml) milk
1 cup (250 ml) heavy cream (36%)
4 egg yolks
¼ cup (60 ml) sugar

PRELIMINARY:
Break the chocolate into squares. Bring the milk and cream to a boil in a saucepan.

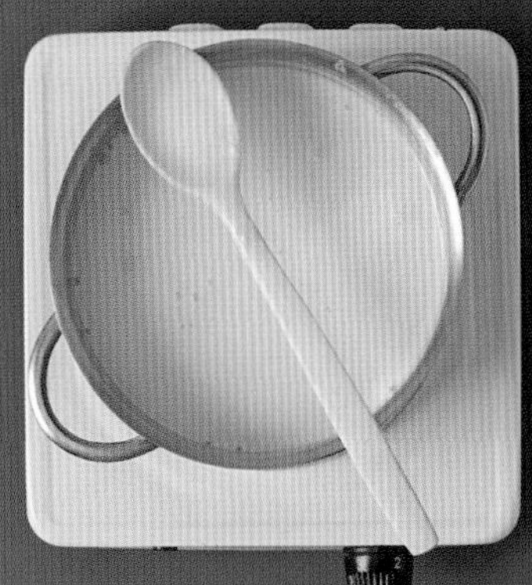

1 2

3 4

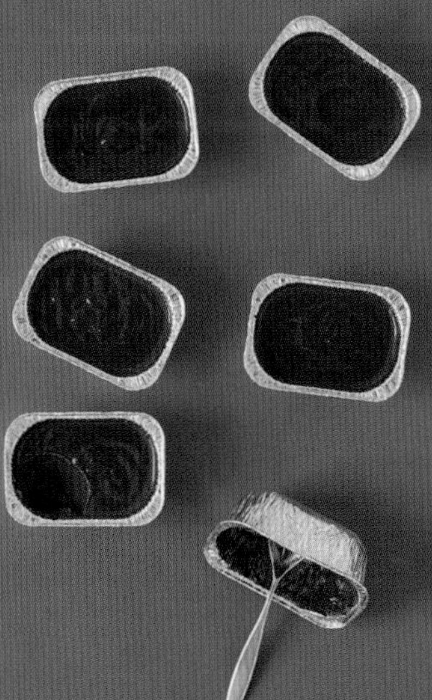

1	Whisk together the egg yolks, sugar and then add a small amount of the milk-cream mixture.	2	Add the sugar mixture to the milk-cream mixture and heat over low heat, stirring. Cook until the mixture thickens and coats a spoon.
3	Pour the hot crème anglaise over the chocolate and whisk together.	4	Once the cream is smooth and uniform, pour into small pots and allow to set in the refrigerator for at least 3 hours.

CHOCOLATE SORBET

YIELD: 4 TO 6 SERVINGS • PREPARATION: 30 MINUTES • BAKING: 5 MINUTES • RESTING: 1 HOUR

2 cups (500 ml) milk
6½ tablespoons (97 ml) sugar
¾ cup (175 ml) cocoa powder
3½ ounces (100 g) dark chocolate morsels (about ½ cup/125 ml)

1 2
3 4

1	Bring the milk, sugar and cocoa powder to a boil.	2	Remove from the heat, add the chocolate and stir until uniform. Set aside in the refrigerator.
3	Once the mixture is cold, about 40°F (4°C), process in an ice cream maker.	4	Serve immediately. If the sorbet is too soft, pour it into a container and allow to set in the freezer for 1 hour.

ICED TIRAMISU IN A GLASS

✦ **YIELD: 4 SERVINGS • PREPARATION: 30 MINUTES • RESTING: 3 HOURS** ✦

FOR THE COFFEE GRANITA:
1 cup (250 ml) strong coffee
3 tablespoons (45 ml) sugar
2 tablespoons (30 ml) cocoa powder

FOR THE MASCARPONE CREAM:
⅔ cup (150 ml) heavy cream (36%)
½ cup (125 ml) confectioners' sugar
2 egg yolks
¼ cup (60 ml) amaretto or Marsala (optional)
9 ounces (250 g) mascarpone
(about 1 cup/250 ml)
1½ tablespoons (22 ml) cocoa powder
1⅔ cups (400 ml) strong coffee
16 ladyfingers

1 2
3 4

1	To prepare the granita, mix the sugar and cocoa with the hot coffee, pour into a shallow dish and allow to set in the freezer.	2	Scrape using a fork and return to the freezer. Repeat several times. The mixture must not solidify or form a solid block.	
3	Using an electric mixer, whip the cream with the confectioners' sugar until stiff.	4	Beat the egg yolks, amaretto and mascarpone, and then whisk in the whipped cream. The cream should be semi-stiff.	➢

5 6

7 8

5	Mix the cocoa with the coffee.	6	Dip ladyfingers in the coffee mixture to soak and place in the bottom of each of 4 glasses.
7	Place a layer of cream on top of the ladyfingers.	8	Repeat steps 6 and 7 twice, ending with a layer of cream. Set aside in the refrigerator for at least 3 hours.

9	To serve, remove the granita from the freezer, scrape with a fork and top the cream with it. Serve immediately.	**TIP** ☛ The tiramisu can be made in a large family-sized dish without the granita.

CRUNCHY AND SOFT

4

PECAN BROWNIES

YIELD: 16 BROWNIES • PREPARATION: 20 MINUTES • BAKING: 35 MINUTES

1 cup (250 ml) butter
12½ ounces (350 g) dark chocolate
3 eggs
1¼ cups (310 ml) brown sugar
⅔ cup (150 ml) flour
1 teaspoon (5 ml) yeast
7 ounces (200 g) pecans, choppped

PRELIMINARY:
Preheat the oven to 325°F (160°C). Butter and flour a square or rectangular baking pan.

1 2

3 4

1	Melt the butter and chocolate together, then set aside.	2	Whisk the eggs and sugar until the mixture is pale.
3	Add the chocolate mixture and combine, then mix in the flour, yeast and nuts.	4	Pour the batter into the pan and bake for about 35 minutes. Allow to cool before cutting.

UNBAKED FRUIT CAKE

YIELD: 8 TO 10 SERVINGS • PREPARATION: 15 MINUTES • RESTING: 2 HOURS

5 ounces (150 g) Dutch spice cookies (speculaas)
1¾ ounces (50 g) meringues
3½ ounces (100 g) dried apricots

7 ounces (200 g) dark chocolate morsels (about 1 cup/250 ml)
3½ ounces (100 g) milk chocolate morsels (about ½ cup/125 ml)

⅔ cup (150 ml) butter
1 tablespoon (15 ml) liquid honey
2 ounces (60 g) dried cranberries
2½ ounces (70 g) pistachios
1¾ ounces (50 g) walnuts

1 2

3 4

1	Using a knife, coarsely chop the cookies, meringues and apricots.	2	Melt the dark and milk chocolate, butter and honey in a microwave oven.
3	Mix the cookies, meringues, dried fruit and nuts. Pour the chocolate mixture on top. Stir well.	4	Pour into a silicone loaf pan and tamp using a spoon. Allow to set in the refrigerator for 2 hours then turn out of the pan.

39

CHOCOLATE-WALNUT COOKIES

YIELD: 25 COOKIES • PREPARATION: 20 MINUTES • BAKING: 10 MINUTES • RESTING: 2 HOURS

1¾ cups (425 ml) flour
½ teaspoon (2 ml) yeast
6 ounces (170 g) dark chocolate or 1 cup (250 ml) dark chocolate morsels
3½ ounces (100 g) walnuts
7 tablespoons (105 ml) butter
1 cup (250 ml) brown sugar
½ teaspoon (2 ml) salt
1 egg
1 teaspoon (5 ml) vanilla extract

PRELIMINARY:
Sift together the flour and yeast.

1 2

3 4

1	Preheat oven to 340°F (170°C). Coarsely chop the chocolate and nuts. Set aside.	2	Work the butter to soften.	
3	Add the sugar and salt to the butter and whisk with an electric mixer until pale.	4	Add the egg and vanilla.	➢

5 6
7 8

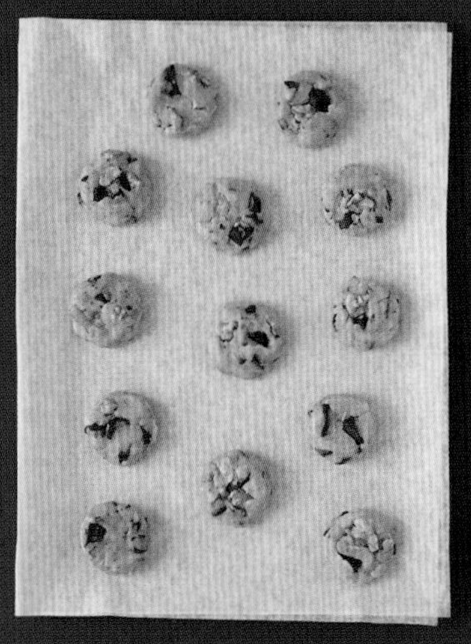

5	Gradually incorporate the flour mixture.	6	Add the chocolate and nut pieces. Mix and allow to rest in the refrigerator for at least 15 minutes.
7	Place small balls of dough on a baking sheet lined with parchment paper.	8	Bake for 10 minutes. The center of the cookies should be soft.

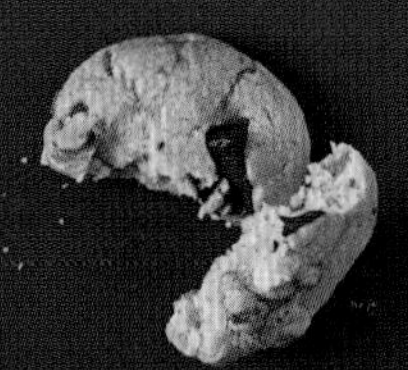

9	Allow the cookies to cool before removing them from the sheet.	**STORAGE** Cookie dough freezes well. Place on plastic wrap and roll, pinching the ends to create a sausage shape. This way, you only have to cut small slices to use. Consider flattening the sides a little to make a more irregular shape.

CHOCOLATE-HAZELNUT COOKIES

VARIATION OF CHOCOLATE-WALNUT COOKIES

Substitute 3½ ounces (100 g) hazelnuts for the walnuts and 6 ounces (170 g) milk chocolate for the dark chocolate. Make the cookies as explained in recipe 39.

CHOCOLATE-MACADAMIA COOKIES

VARIATION OF CHOCOLATE-WALNUT COOKIES

Substitute 3½ ounces (100 g) white chocolate for the dark chocolate and 3 ounces (80 g) macadamia nuts or blanched almonds for the walnuts. Make the cookies as explained in recipe 39.

HAZELNUT CRUMBLE CHOCOLATE MOUSSE

YIELD: 12 SERVINGS • PREPARATION: 35 MINUTES • BAKING: 20 MINUTES • RESTING: 5 HOURS

FOR THE CRUST:

4½ ounces (125 g) good-quality wafer cookies
7 ounces (200 g) hazelnut-flavored milk chocolate

FOR THE CRÈME ANGLAISE:

1 cup (250 ml) milk
3 egg yolks
1 tablespoon (15 ml) sugar
1 vanilla bean

FOR THE CHOCOLATE MOUSSE:

10½ ounces (300 g) milk chocolate morsels (about 1½ cups/375 ml)
1 cup (250 ml) heavy cream (36%) , cold

FOR THE HAZELNUT CRUMBLE:

⅔ cup (150 ml) flour
6½ tablespoons (97 ml) sugar
6 tablespoons (90 ml) butter, softened
2 ounces (60 g) hazelnuts, ground

PRELIMINARY:

Crush the wafers between your hands. Melt the hazelnut-flavored milk chocolate.

1	Prepare the crème anglaise (see recipe 2): pour the milk over the egg yolk, sugar and vanilla mixture. Cook until the cream thickens.	2	Pour ⅔ cup (150 ml) hot crème anglaise over the milk chocolate, wait 2 minutes and then mix. Allow to cool.	
3	With an electric mixer, whip the cold cream until stiff, then fold into the cooled chocolate mixture.	4	Pour the chocolate mousse into a silicone loaf pan. Freeze for at least 4 hours.	➢

5	Place all the crumble ingredients in a bowl. Combine using your hands until it forms large crumbs, or use a food processor.	6	Transfer to a baking sheet and bake in a 350°F (180°C) oven until golden (15 to 20 minutes). Set aside.
7	Pour the melted hazelnut–milk chocolate over the crushed wafers. Stir to completely coat the wafers.	8	Once the mousse loaf has set, pour the coated wafers on top, gently press in with a spoon and store in the refrigerator.

To serve, turn the chilled mousse out onto a dish and top with the hazelnut crumble.

TIP

☛ Individual portions can be prepared in a silicone muffin pan. To turn them out of the pan, place a board on top of the pan and turn upside down in one movement.

PINWHEEL COOKIES

YIELD: 40 COOKIES • PREPARATION: 30 MINUTES • BAKING: 20 MINUTES • RESTING: 15 MINUTES

½ cup (125 ml) butter
1⅛ cup (280 ml) confectioners' sugar
1 teaspoon (5 ml) vanilla extract
1 egg

2 cups (500 ml) flour
3 tablespoons (45 ml) cocoa powder, sifted
½ cup (125 ml) granulated sugar

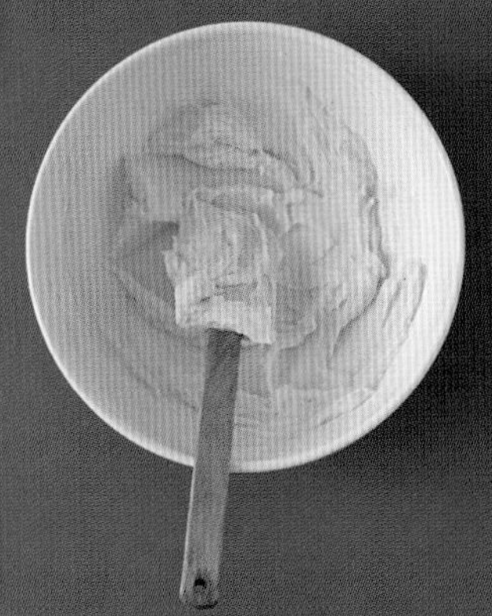

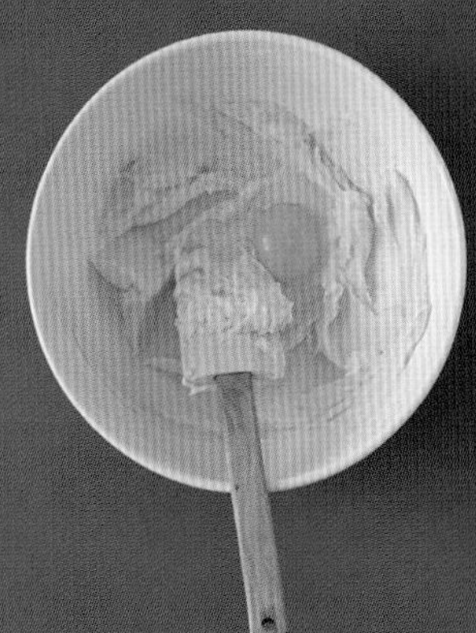

1 2

3 4

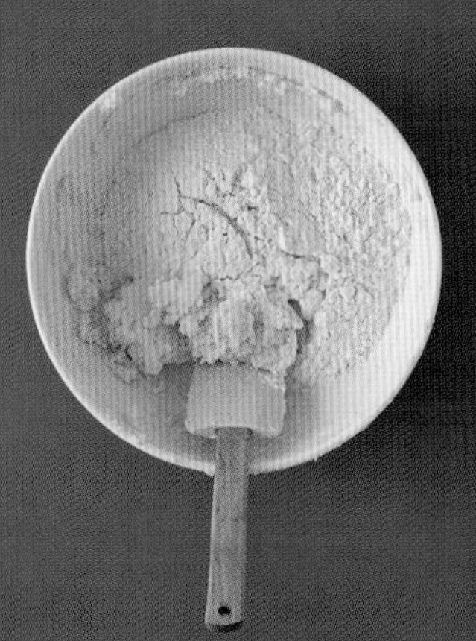

1	Work the butter with the confectioners' sugar and vanilla until softened.	2	Add the egg and mix until the dough is uniform.	
3	Add the flour and mix until the dough forms a ball; do not overwork.	4	Divide the dough ball in half. Mix the cocoa into one half. Set the two dough balls aside in the refrigerator for 15 minutes.	➢

5 6
7 8

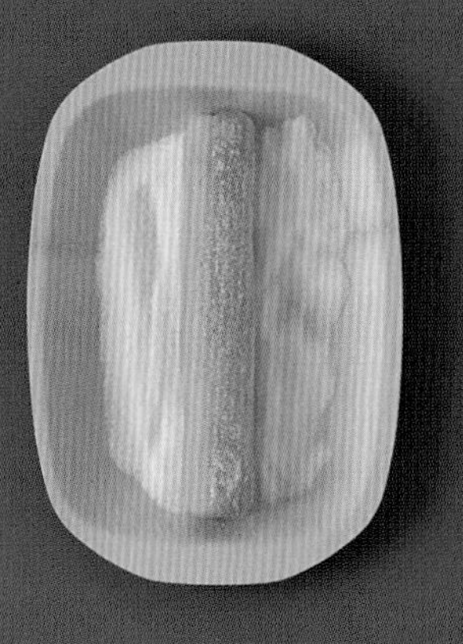

5	Roll the white dough out to a thickness of 1/16 inch (2 or 3 mm) to form an 8¼- × 6-inch (21 × 15 cm) rectangle. Roll out the cocoa dough into an 8- × 5¾-inch (20.5 × 14.5 cm) rectangle.	6	Lay the cocoa dough rectangle on the white dough rectangle lengthwise, and roll without leaving any space between the two doughs.
7	Roll the dough in the granulated sugar.	8	Next, cut slices about 1/16 inch (3 mm) thick. Place on a baking sheet lined with parchment paper.

9	Bake in a 350°F (180°C) oven until slightly golden, about 15 to 20 minutes. Cool before eating.	**TIP** ☛ Use a sheet of legal-sized paper folded in half to form rectangles of the right size.

VIENNESE MINI SHORTBREAD COOKIES

YIELD: 25 COOKIES • PREPARATION: 20 MINUTES • BAKING: 12 MINUTES

¾ cup (175 ml) butter
1½ cups (375 ml) flour
1 pinch salt

3 tablespoons (45 ml) cocoa powder
1 egg
⅔ cup (150 ml) confectioners' sugar

PRELIMINARY:
Work the butter until softened and smooth. Sift together the flour, salt and cocoa.

1 2

3 4

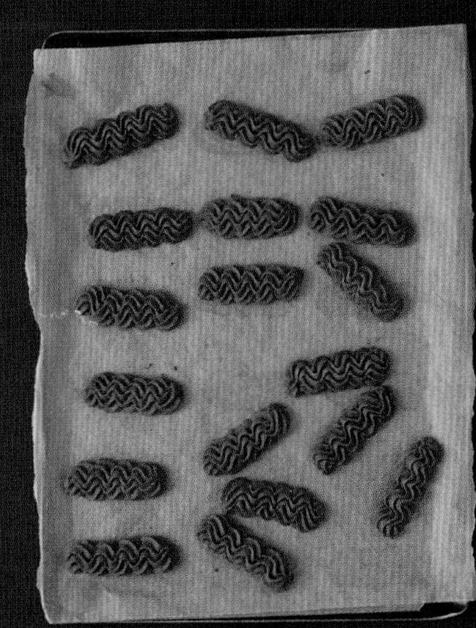

1	Lightly beat the egg along with the confectioners' sugar. Mix in with the butter.	2	Gradually mix in the flour mixture.
3	Put the dough in a pastry bag fitted with a fluted tip. Create the shortbread cookies by piping 3 consecutive Ws on a baking sheet lined with parchment paper.	4	Bake in a 340°F (170°C) oven for 12 minutes.

45

DOUBLE CHOCOLATE BAR

YIELD: AN APPROX. 3-POUND (1.5 KG) BAR • PREPARATION: 10 MINUTES • RESTING: 40 MINUTES

12 ounces (340 g) milk chocolate
6½ ounces (180 g) white chocolate
¾ cup (175 ml) puffed rice cereal

1 2

3 4

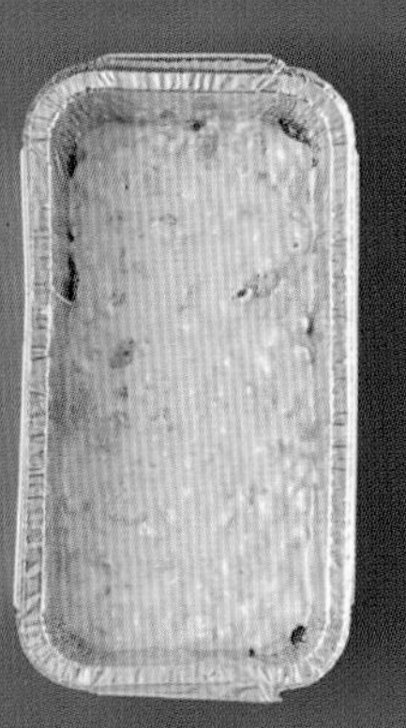

1	Melt half the milk chocolate in a microwave oven or double boiler. Pour into a $7\frac{1}{2}$- × $3\frac{3}{4}$-inch (19 × 9 cm) aluminum loaf pan and chill in the refrigerator for 5 minutes.	2	Melt the white chocolate in a microwave oven or double boiler. Add the puffed rice and stir.
3	Pour over the cooled milk chocolate. Chill for 5 minutes.	4	Melt the remaining milk chocolate and pour over the chilled white chocolate. Set aside in the refrigerator. Once the chocolate has hardened, turn out of the pan.

PUFFED RICE BAR

VARIATION OF DOUBLE CHOCOLATE BAR

Melt 9½ ounces (270 g) chocolate in a double boiler or microwave oven. Mix in 1 cup (250 ml) puffed rice cereal, then pour into a loaf pan. Allow to set in a cool location. Turn out of the pan once the chocolate has hardened.

"EVERYTHING I LOVE" BAR

VARIATION OF DOUBLE CHOCOLATE BAR

Melt 9½ ounces (270 g) dark chocolate. Incorporate a mixture of dried fruits and nuts (almonds, hazelnuts, raisins, apricots, figs), then pour into a loaf pan.

The possibilities are endless: you can add whatever you like, such as marshmallows, nougat, marzipan, caramels, etc.

CHOCOLATE PIE

YIELD: 6 SERVINGS • PREPARATION: 15 MINUTES • BAKING: 20 MINUTES • RESTING: 2 HOURS

1 batch sugar pastry (see recipe 5)
6½ ounces (180 g) 64% cocoa chocolate morsels (about ⅞ cup/210 ml)
1 ounce (30 g) milk chocolate morsels (about 2½ tablespoons/37 ml)
1 cup (250 ml) heavy cream (36%)
1 vanilla bean

1	Roll out the dough and place in a buttered 9-inch (23 cm) non-stick pie plate. Prick the bottom with a fork, then freeze for 15 minutes.	2	Line the chilled crust with parchment paper, fill with dried beans and bake for 20 minutes. Turn out of the pan and allow to cool on a rack.
3	Prepare a ganache (see recipe 8), adding a halved vanilla bean with the seeds scraped out to the cream.	4	Pour the still-warm ganache into the bottom of the cold piecrust and allow to set at room temperature or, to speed things up, place the pie in the refrigerator.

CHOCOLATE-CARAMEL PIE

YIELD: 6 TO 8 SERVINGS • PREPARATION: 30 MINUTES • BAKING: 20 MINUTES • RESTING: 2 HOURS

1 batch sugar pastry (see recipe 5)

FOR THE CARAMEL:

⅔ cup (150 ml) heavy cream (36%)
¾ cup (175 ml) sugar
1 tablespoon (15 ml) salted butter

FOR THE GANACHE:

⅔ cup (150 ml) heavy cream (36%)
6½ ounces (180 g) dark chocolate

PRELIMINARY:

Roll out the dough, place in a buttered rectangular tart tin and freeze for 15 minutes. Preheat the oven to 350°F (180°C).

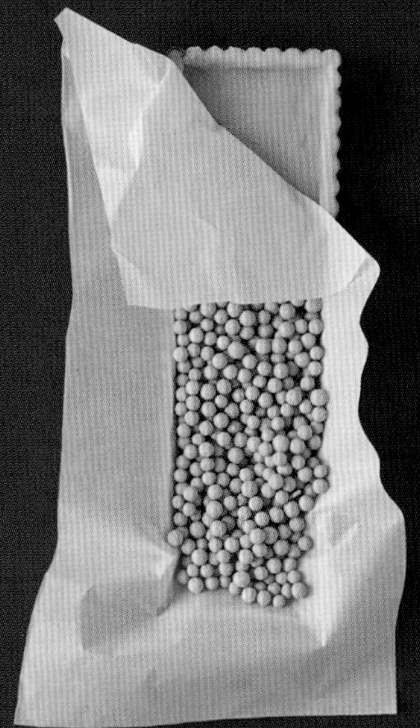

1 2

3 4

1	Line the dough with parchment paper, fill with dried beans and bake for 20 minutes.	2	To make the caramel, heat the ⅔ cup (150 ml) cream. Next place the sugar and 1 tablespoon (15 ml) water in a separate saucepan. Heat until it becomes a lovely amber-colored caramel.	
3	Remove from the heat, place over the sink and carefully add the hot cream. Watch out for any bubbling or spills.	4	Place back on the heat and add the salted butter. Cook for another minute. Allow to cool.	➢

49

5 6
7 8

5	Pour the caramel into the cold piecrust. Allow to harden.	6	Meanwhile, heat the ⅔ cup (150 ml) cream to prepare the ganache (see recipe 8).
7	Pour the hot cream over the chocolate, wait 2 minutes and then mix to obtain a smooth and uniform ganache.	8	Once the caramel has slightly hardened, cover with ganache.

		VARIATION
9	Set aside in the refrigerator until ready to serve.	☛ The pie can also be prepared using cocoa sugar pastry (see recipe 5).

CARAMEL-NUT TARTLETS

YIELD: 12 TARTS • PREPARATION: 35 MINUTES • BAKING: 15 MINUTES

FOR THE COCOA SUGAR PASTRY:
⅔ cup (150 ml) butter
½ cup (125 ml) sugar
1 egg
1⅔ cups (400 ml) flour
½ cup (125 ml) ground almonds
1½ tablespoons (22 ml) cocoa powder
1 teaspoon (5 ml) vanilla extract

FOR THE NUT CARAMEL:
1½ ounces (35 g) walnuts
1½ ounces (35 g) pine nuts
1½ ounces (35 g) pistachios
⅓ cup (75 ml) heavy cream (36%)
½ cup (125 ml) sugar
1 tablespoon (15 ml) water

PRELIMINARY:
Preheat the oven to 350°F (180°C).

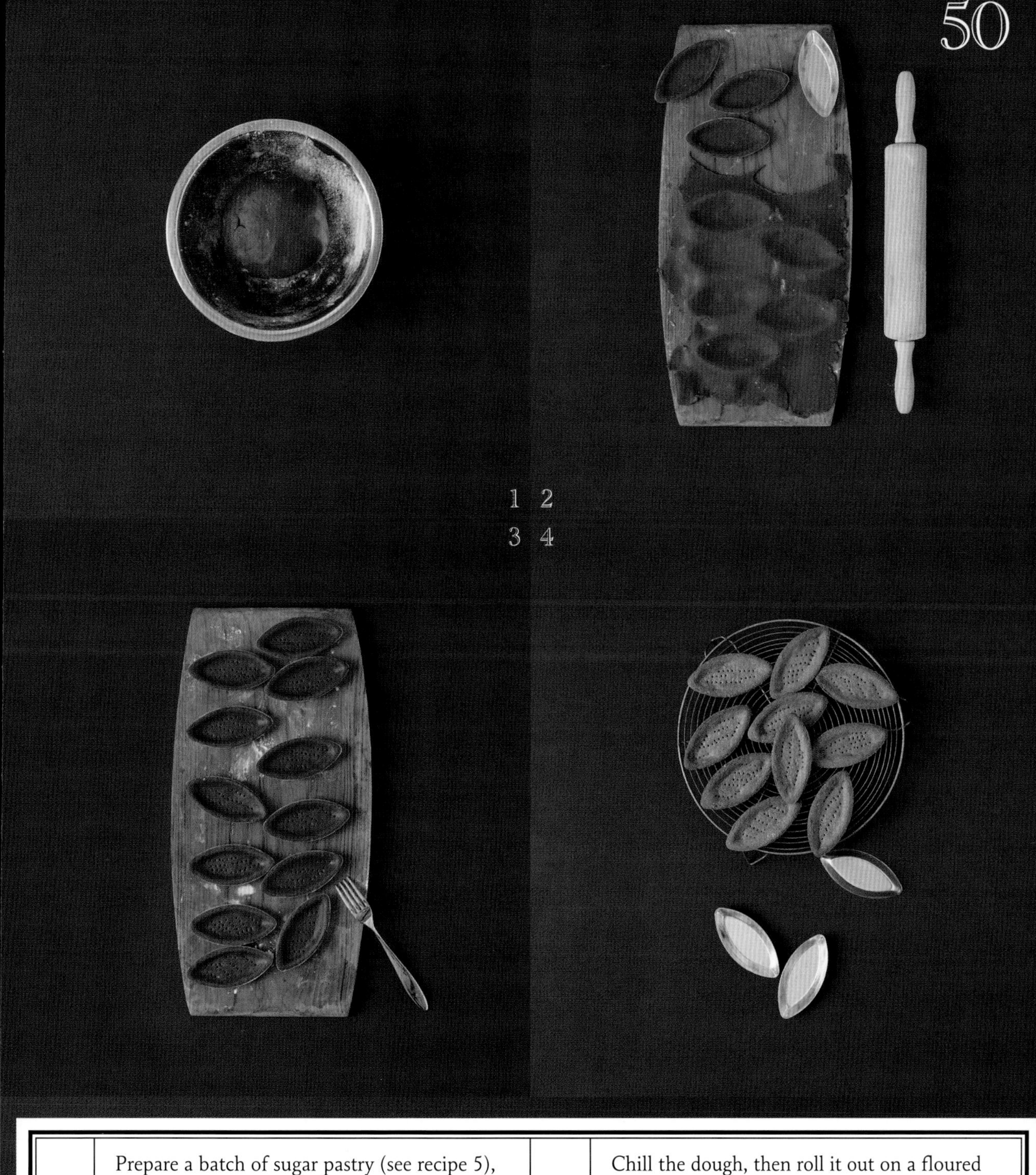

1	Prepare a batch of sugar pastry (see recipe 5), incorporating the cocoa at the same time as the flour.	2	Chill the dough, then roll it out on a floured work surface. Cover mini tart pans with the dough and, using a rolling pin, press to divide up the dough. Remove any excess dough. Using your fingers, press the dough into the pans.	
3	Prick the bottom of each with a fork and bake for 15 minutes.	4	Turn the tartlets out of the pan and allow to cool on a rack.	➢

5	Coarsely chop the nuts.	6	Transfer to a dish and place in a warm oven, with the heat turned off. Stir occasionally.
7	Heat the cream. Meanwhile, place the sugar and water in another pot. Heat until it becomes a nice amber-colored caramel.	8	Remove the caramel from the heat, place over the sink and carefully pour in the hot cream. Watch out for bubbling and spills. Stir, then add the nuts.

9	Fill the tartlet crusts with the caramel mixture.	**STORAGE** You can use this recipe to make a large pie. Don't roll out the dough too thinly, as there must be a reasonable thickness to maintain a balance between the caramel and the pastry.

CAKES

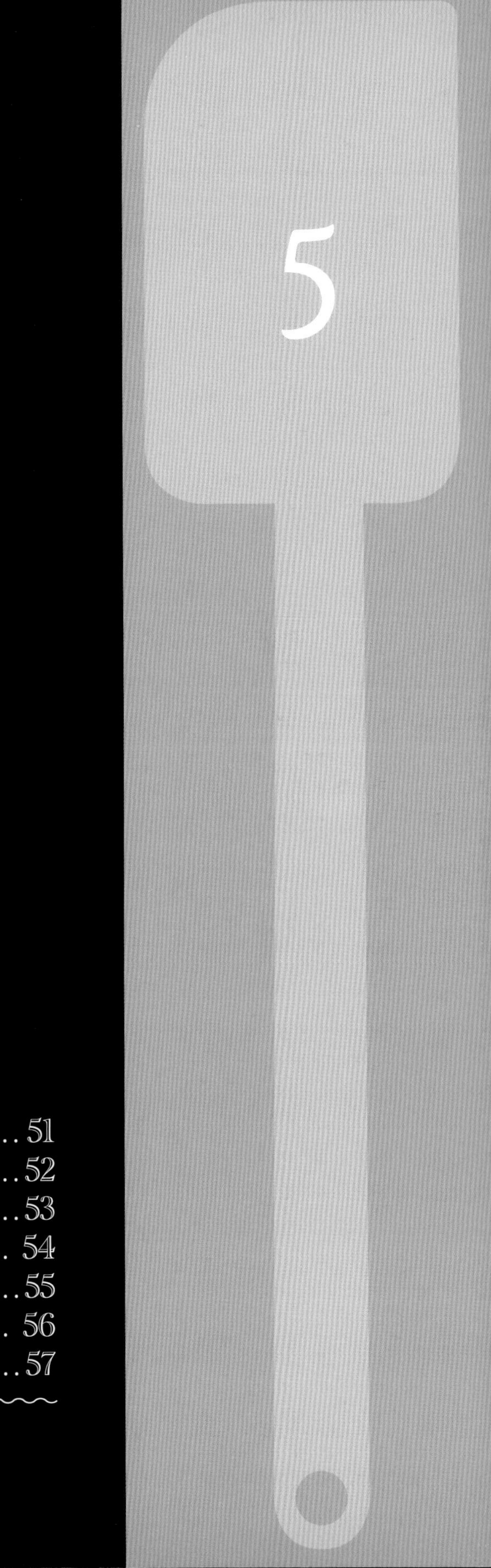
5

CHOCOLATE YULE LOG

YIELD: 6 SERVINGS • PREPARATION: 50 MINUTES • BAKING: 5 MINUTES • RESTING: 2 HOURS

FOR THE CAKE:

3 eggs
¼ cup (60 ml) flour
2 tablespoons (30 ml) cornstarch
¼ cup (60 ml) cocoa powder
¼ cup (60 ml) sugar

FOR THE MOUSSE:

5 ounces (150 g) dark chcolate
1¼ cups (310 ml) heavy cream (36%)

FOR THE SYRUP:

3 pear halves in syrup
7 tablespoons (105 ml) pear syrup
1 tablespoon (15 ml) pear brandy (optional)

TO DECORATE (OPTIONAL):

5 ounces (150 g) dark chocolate

PRELIMINARY:

Preheat the oven to 400°F (200°C).
Separate the egg whites from the yolks.

1 2 3

4 5 6

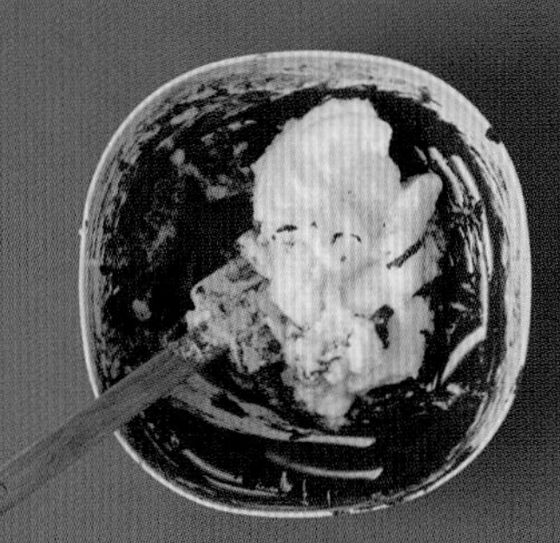

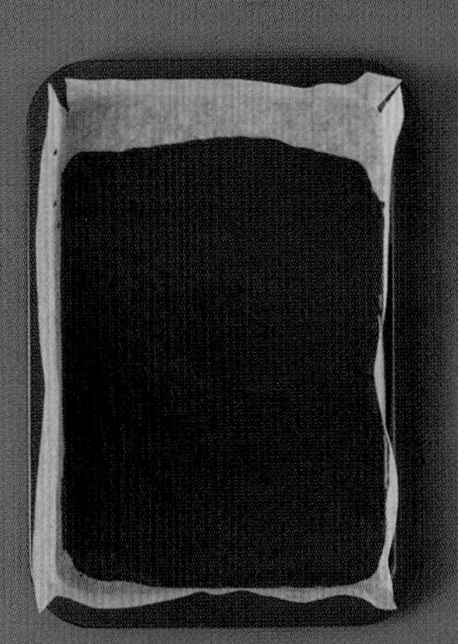

1	Sift together the flour, cornstarch and cocoa.	2	Beat the egg yolks along with the sugar.	3	Add the flour mixture and lightly whisk.	
4	With an electric mixer, whisk the egg whites until stiff and then carefully fold into the mixture.	5	Pour onto a 13- × 9-inch (33 × 23 cm) baking pan lined with parchment paper and bake for 5 to 7 minutes.	6	Turn the cake out of the pan when still hot. Set aside.	➢

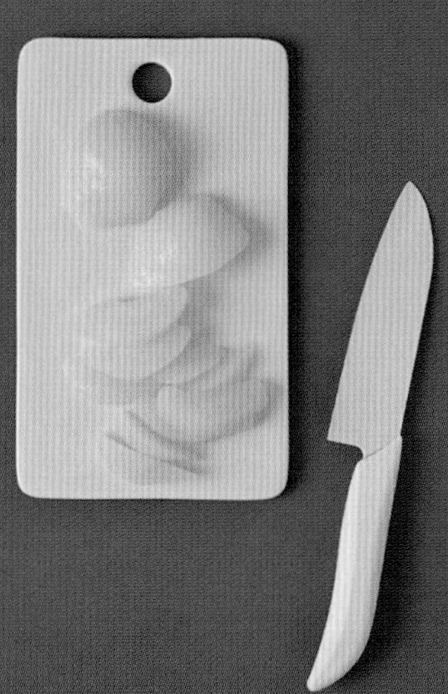

7	Prepare a ganache (see recipe 8) using the chocolate and ⅔ cup (150 ml) heavy cream.	8	Whip the remaining cream until stiff.
9	Fold the whipped cream into the ganache to make a mousse.	10	Slice the pear halves into strips.

11 12

13 14

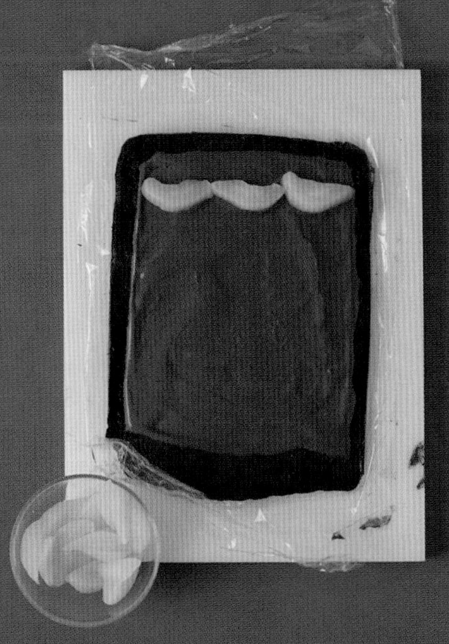

11	Place the cooled cake onto a piece of plastic wrap. Soak it with syrup.	12	Pour half of the mousse onto the cake. Spread using a spatula, leaving a ½-inch (1 cm) margin along the sides and a 1-inch (3 cm) margin at the ends.	
13	Arrange the pear strips on the mousse.	14	Roll up the yule log, wrap in plastic wrap and allow to set in the refrigerator for at least 1 hour.	➢

15 16
17 18

15	Remove the log from the refrigerator. Soak the top with syrup. Ice with the remaining mousse. Return to the refrigerator for 20 minutes.	16	To decorate, melt the chocolate. Fold a large sheet of parchment paper in half. Spread the chocolate over half of the sheet. Fold again and smooth using a spatula. Allow to harden in a cool place for 30 minutes.
17	Once the chocolate is hard, break into irregularly shaped chunks to create pieces of bark.	18	Slice both ends of the chilled yule log and transfer it to a dish. Arrange the pieces of bark, starting at the bottom and working toward the top.

19	It's ready! Serve in thick slices.

VARIATION

☛ The log can be decorated using a mixture of pears and chestnuts. In this case, substitute cognac or whiskey for the pear brandy.

TIP

The log can be prepared 2 days in advance. In this case, only prepare half of the mousse, for use as the filling. Prepare the second half, to ice the log, and the chocolate bark a few hours before serving.

AUTUMN LAYERS

YIELD: 8 TO 10 SERVINGS • PREPARATION: 45 MINUTES • BAKING: 2½ HOURS • RESTING: 2 HOURS

FOR THE MERINGUE:

4 egg whites (about ½ cup/125 ml)
½ cup (125 ml) superfine sugar
1 teaspoon (5 ml) vanilla extract
1 teaspoon (5 ml) confectioners' sugar, sifted

FOR THE CHOCOLATE MOUSSE:

7 tablespoons (105 ml) milk
10½ ounces (300 g) dark chocolate
3 egg yolks
3 tablespoons (45 ml) butter, softened
6 egg whites

PRELIMINARY:

Using the bottom of a 9-inch (23 cm) diameter pie plate as a guide, trace three 8½-inch (21.5 cm) diameter circles on two sheets of parchment paper. Set aside. Preheat the oven to 250°F (120°C).

1 2

3 4

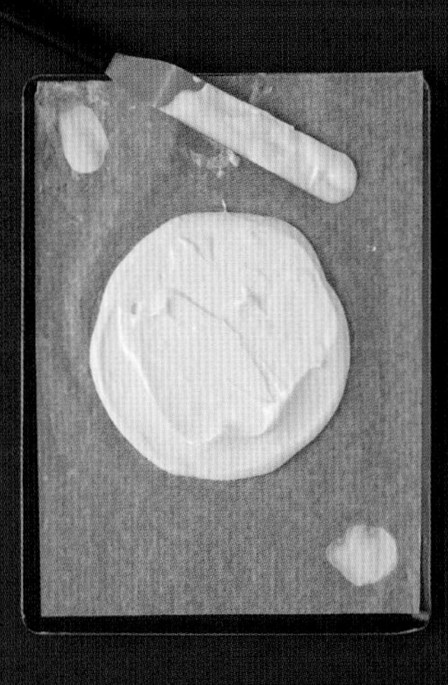

1	Using an electric mixer, whisk the 4 egg whites until stiff, gradually adding the superfine sugar in 3 batches.	2	Once the egg whites are stiff and shiny, add the vanilla and fold in the confectioners' sugar using a spatula.
3	Pour a third of the egg white mixture onto one of the parchment-paper circles and spread uniformly using a spatula.	4	Repeat this step with the other circles. Make sure the egg whites are spread thinly, about ½ inch (1 cm) thick. Bake for 2½ hours. Let cool. ➢

5	Prepare an egg mousse (see recipe 6) by pouring hot milk over the chocolate, then adding the egg yolks.	6	Work the butter with a spatula until softened.
7	Gradually whisk the softened butter into the chocolate mixture.	8	Whisk the egg whites with an electric mixer until stiff. Fold into the chocolate mixture.

Cover the inside of a baking pan with plastic wrap, taking care to go beyond the sides.

10	Pour a little chocolate mousse into the pan.	11	Position a meringue disk flat side up on top of the mousse (the uneven side will be on the mousse).
12	Cover the meringue with mousse, then position the second disk on top. Carefully press, forcing some mousse to squeeze out.	13	Once again, cover with mousse and finish with the last meringue disk. Allow to set in the freezer for 1 hour.

14

Turn the cake out by pulling the sides of the plastic wrap. Refrigerate for about 1 hour, until the cake reaches refrigerator temperature.

DECORATION

Use ganache (see recipe 8), fancy icing (see recipe 9) or chocolate shavings (see recipe 12) to decorate the cake.

WHITE FOREST CAKE

YIELD: 8 TO 10 SERVINGS • PREPARATION: 45 MINUTES • BAKING: 35 MINUTES • RESTING: 3 HOURS

FOR THE CAKE:
6 egg yolks
⅔ cup (150 ml) superfine sugar
2½ tablespoons (37 ml) all-purpose flour
3 tablespoons (45 ml) potato flour
7 tablespoon (105 ml) cocoa powder
6 egg whites

FOR THE CHOCOLATE MOUSSE:
7 ounces (200 g) dark chocolate
7 tablespoons (105 ml) milk
1 cup (250 ml) heavy cream (36%)

FOR THE GARNISH:
14 ounces (400 g) amarena cherries in syrup
1 cup (250 ml) cherry syrup
3 tablespoons (45 ml) kirsch

FOR THE WHIPPED CREAM:
1¼ cups (310 ml) heavy cream (36%)
¼ cup (60 ml) confectioners' sugar
1 tablespoon (15 ml) vanilla extract

FOR THE DECORATION (OPTIONAL):
8 cherries with stems
2½ ounces (70 g) white chocolate morsels (about ⅓ cup/75 ml)

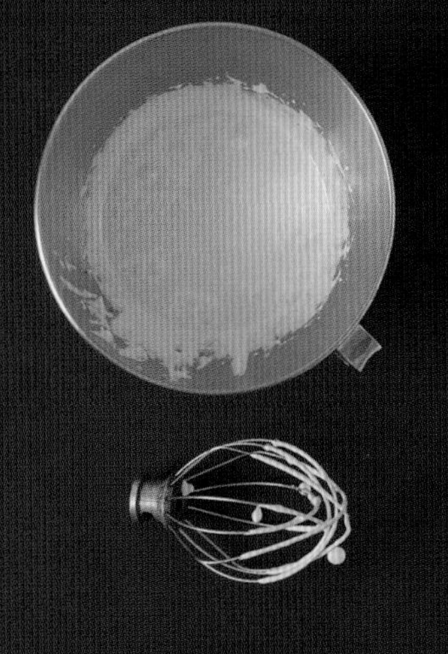

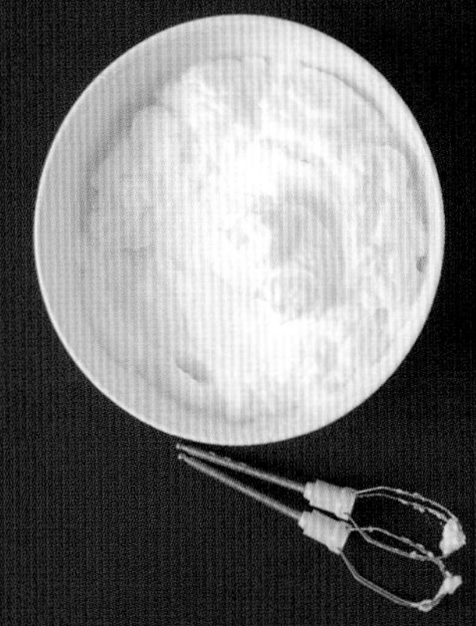

1 2 3

4 5 6

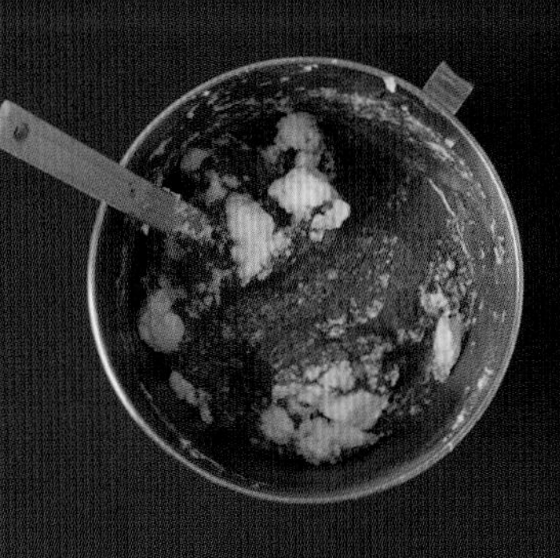

1	With an electric mixer, whisk the egg yolks with the sugar.	2	Once the mixture is very foamy, fold in the all-purpose flour, potato flour and cocoa.	3	Whisk the egg whites with an electric mixer until stiff.
4	Carefully fold the egg whites into the flour mixture.	5	Pour into a buttered and floured round baking pan and bake in a 350°F (180°C) oven for 35 minutes.	6	Turn the cake out of the hot pan and allow to cool before slicing it into three layers. ➢

7 8
9 10

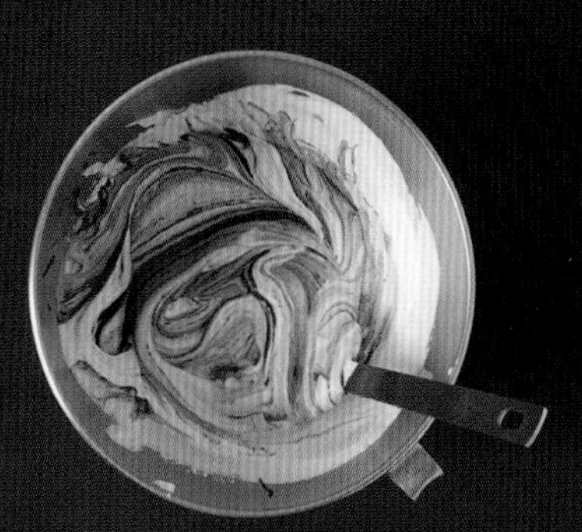

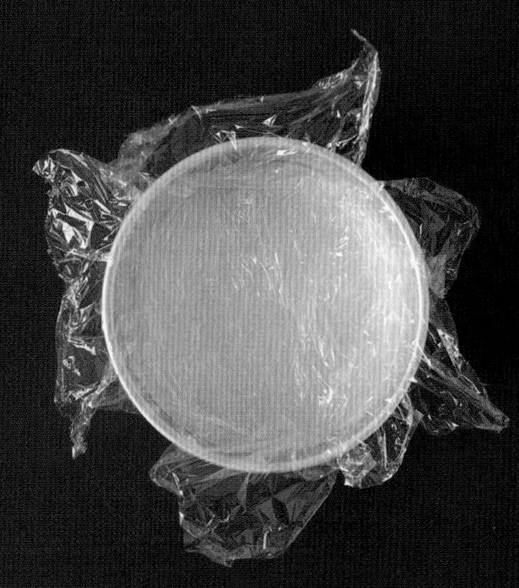

7	To make the chocolate mousse, melt the chocolate and milk in a double boiler or microwave oven.	8	Whip the cream with an electric mixer until stiff.
9	Carefully fold the cream into the warm chocolate.	10	Line the pan used to bake the cake with plastic wrap.

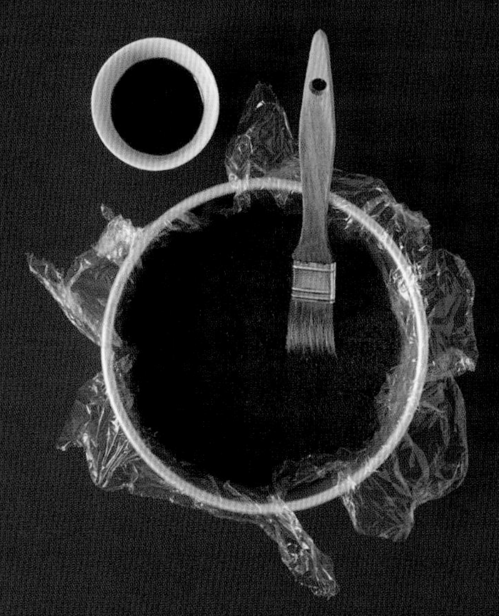

11 12

13 14

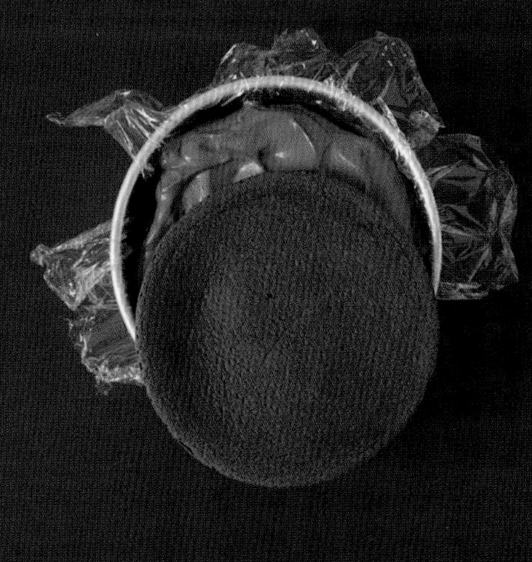

11	Place the top of the cake in the bottom of the pan. Generously soak with cherry syrup (with the kirsch added or not).	12	Sprinkle amarena cherries and spread half of the chocolate mousse on top.	
13	Position the second cake disk and press down lightly. Soak with syrup, sprinkle the rest of the cherries and spread the rest of the mousse on top.	14	Fold the ends of the plastic wrap over the cake and allow to set in the freezer for 2 hours.	➢

15 16
17 18

15	For the decoration, melt the white chocolate in a microwave oven, dip the cherries into the chocolate and set aside on parchment paper.	16	For the whipped cream, whip the cream with the confectioners' sugar and vanilla extract.
17	Remove the cake from the freezer and turn it out of the pan. Ice with the whipped cream, using a spatula to cover the entire cake.	18	Using a pastry bag with a fluted tip, create 8 rosettes.

19 Carefully arrange the white chocolate cherries on the rosettes. Refrigerate for at least 1 hour before serving.

BANANA SPLIT CAKE

YIELD: 10 TO 12 SERVINGS • PREPARATION: 45 MINUTES • BAKING: 25 MINUTES • RESTING: 1 HOUR

1 genoise (see recipe 4) baked with:
6 eggs
¾ cup (175 ml) sugar
½ cup + 1 tablespoon (140 ml) flour
6 tablespoons (90 ml) cornstarch
½ cup (125 ml) ground almonds
¼ cup (60 ml) cocoa powder

FOR THE SYRUP:
2 vanilla beans
⅓ cup (75 ml) sugar
½ cup (125 ml) water

FOR THE GARNISH:
3 ounces (80 g) chocolate
2 cups (500 ml) heavy cream (36%)
6½ tablespoons (97 ml) confectioners' sugar
3 bananas
½ lemon

PRELIMINARY:
Preheat the oven to 350°F (180°C). Slice the genoise into three layers.

1 2

3 4

1	Halve the 2 vanilla beans and scrape out the seeds. Save the seeds for the whipped cream.	2	Place the empty beans along with the sugar in water in a saucepan. Heat to melt the sugar and make a syrup. Set aside.	
3	Using a peeler, make small chocolate shavings by scraping the end of the chocolate bar (see recipe 12). Set aside in the refrigerator.	4	In a cold bowl, whip the cream, confectioners' sugar and vanilla seeds with an electric mixer until the cream is stiff.	➢

5 6
7 8

5	Slice the bananas and roll the slices in the lemon juice to prevent them from turning brown.	6	Generously soak the base of the genoise with the syrup.
7	Spread a third of the whipped cream onto the cake base using a spatula. Arrange half of the banana slices and sprinkle chocolate shavings on top.	8	Cover with the second layer of genoise and repeat steps 6 and 7.

9	Finish building the cake by adding the remaining third of whipped cream and the rest of the chocolate shavings. Refrigerate for at least 1 hour.

TIP

☛ Do not make this cake too far in advance because the whipped cream and sliced bananas will not keep for more than a day.

ACCOMPANIMENT

Contrary to what one might think, this cake is extremely light. It can be served with a dish of vanilla ice cream and chocolate sauce (see recipe 27).

SERVING SUGGESTION

☛ Cut thick slices — even if it means sharing one slice between two of you on the same plate!

GIRLS' CAKE

YIELD: 8 TO 10 SERVINGS • PREPARATION: 40 MINUTES • BAKING: 30 MINUTES • RESTING: 2 HOURS

1 genoise (see recipe 4) baked with:
4 eggs
⅔ cup (150 ml) sugar
½ cup + 1 tablespoon (140 ml) flour
⅔ cup (150 ml) ground almonds
2 tablespoons (30 ml) butter
Pinch salt

FOR THE SYRUP:
⅓ cup (75 ml) sugar
¼ cup (60 ml) grenadine

FOR THE GARNISH:
2½ cups (625 ml) heavy cream (36%)
3 ounces (90 g) white chocolate, chopped
1 tablespoon (15 ml) sugar
Red food coloring
9 ounces (250 g) raspberries (about 1¾ cups/325 ml)
8 to 10 white chocolate hearts

PRELIMINARY:
Slice the genoise into two layers.

1 2
3 4

1	Prepare the syrup by heating ½ cup (125 ml) water and the sugar. Add the grenadine and let cool.	2	Bring ½ cup (125 ml) of the cream to the boil. Pour the hot cream over the white chocolate. Whisk until the chocolate melts. Set aside.
3	With an electric mixer, whip the rest of the cream in a cold bowl until stiff. Remove half and fold into the white chocolate mixture.	4	Add the sugar and a few drops of food coloring to the other half of the whipped cream, beating to ensure the color is even. ➢

5 6

7 8

5	Soak cut side of the bottom layer of the genoise with syrup.	6	Spread half of the white chocolate on top and sprinkle raspberries over.
7	Cover with the rest of the white chocolate mixture.	8	Soak the cut side of the other genoise layer and place on top of the cake. Soak the top of the cake again and completely cover with the pink whipped cream.

9

Decorate with the rest of the raspberries and the white chocolate hearts. Refrigerate for at least 2 hours before serving.

SACHERTORTE

YIELD: 8 SERVINGS • PREPARATION: 45 MINUTES • BAKING: 25 MINUTES • RESTING: 2 HOURS, 45 MINUTES

FOR THE APRICOT COMPOTE:
10½ ounces (300 g) fresh (or frozen) apricots
6½ tablespoons (97 ml) sugar

FOR THE CAKE:
4 eggs
½ cup (125 ml) sugar
⅓ cup (75 ml) cocoa powder
2 tablespoons (30 ml) potato flour

FOR THE GANACHE:
9 ounces (250 g) dark chocolate
1 cup (250 ml) heavy cream (36%)

PRELIMINARY:
Preheat the oven to 350°F (180°C). Coarsely chop the apricots.

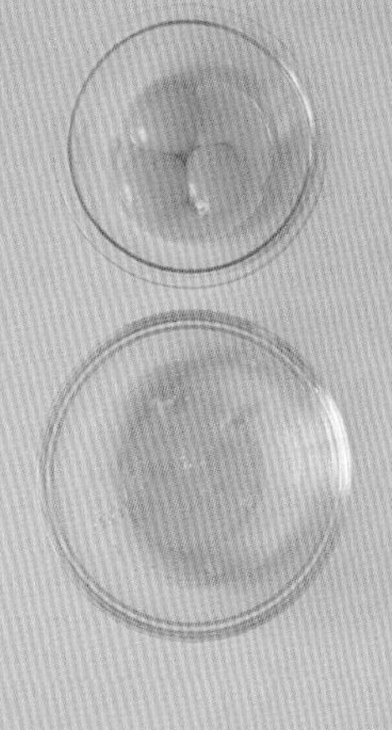

1 2 3

4 5 6

1	Simmer the apricots with the sugar and 2 tablespoons (30 ml) water for 5 minutes.	2	Pour into a strainer over a bowl to drain the syrup. Set the cooked apricots and syrup aside.	3	Separate the egg whites from the yolks.
4	Using an electric mixer, beat the yolks with 1½ tablespoons (22 ml) sugar until the mixture becomes pale.	5	Whisk the whites with an electric mixer until stiff, gradually adding the remaining sugar.	6	Carefully fold the yolks into the whites. ➢

7 8
9 10

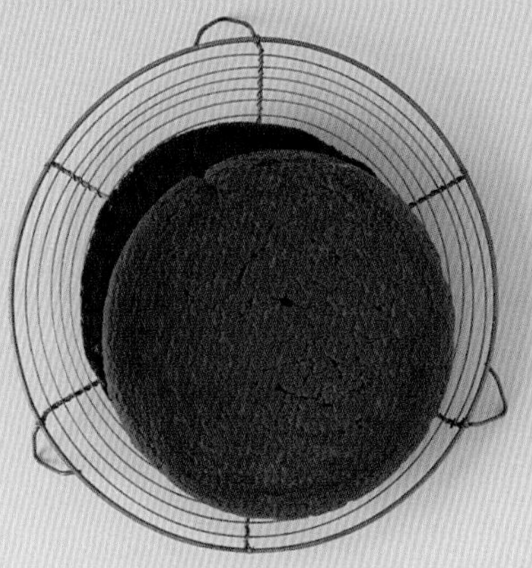

7	Fold the cocoa and potato flour into the egg mixture.	8	Pour the batter into a buttered and floured 8-inch (20 cm) diameter cake pan.
9	Bake for 20 minutes. Turn the cake out of the pan and allow to cool before cutting it in half to make two layers.	10	Prepare the ganache (see recipe 8) using the chocolate and cream.

11 12
13 14

11	Using plastic wrap, line the pan used to bake the cake and pour in a little ganache.	12	Position the top layer of the cake on top of the ganache. Soak well with syrup, then pour a thin laycr of ganache over. Set aside the rest of the ganache (for the icing).	
13	Spread the apricot compote over the ganache layer.	14	Soak the cut side of the other half of the cake with the remaining syrup and seal the cake, pressing lightly. Refrigerate for 2 hours.	➢

15

Remove the cake from the refrigerator. If the ganache is too thick, reheat it quickly in a microwave oven. Turn the Sachertorte out onto a rack by pulling on the sides of the plastic wrap. Pour the ganache over top and smooth using a small spatula. Refrigerate for about 45 minutes.

TIP

☛ To make the cake shiny, use fancy icing (see recipe 9). Once the ganache has set, pour the fancy icing over top and store in the refrigerator until ready to serve.

16	Once the ganache has set, transfer the cake to a dish.	**TIP** ☛ The Sachertorte will taste better if it's prepared in the morning for that evening or, better still, the day before for the next day.

WALNUT CAKE

YIELD: 12 SERVINGS • PREPARATION: 50 MINUTES • BAKING: 50 MINUTES • RESTING: 1 HOUR

FOR THE GROUND WALNUT CAKE:
8 eggs • 7 ounces (200 g) walnuts, ground
½ cup (125 ml) sugar
½ cup + 1 tablespoon (140 ml) flour

FOR THE CHOPPED WALNUT CAKE:
6 egg whites
6½ tablespoons (97 ml) sugar
¼ cup + 2 tablespoons (90 ml) flour
5 ounces (150 g) walnuts, coarsely chopped

FOR THE CHOCOLATE CREAM:
6 egg yolks
3¼ cups (810 ml) confectioners' sugar
14 ounces (400 g) dark chocolate
1¾ cups (325 ml) butter, softened

FOR THE SYRUP:
½ cup (125 ml) sugar
1 tablespoon (15 ml) coffee extract

PRELIMINARY:
Prepare the syrup by heating 1 cup (250 ml) water with the sugar. Add the coffee extract and mix.

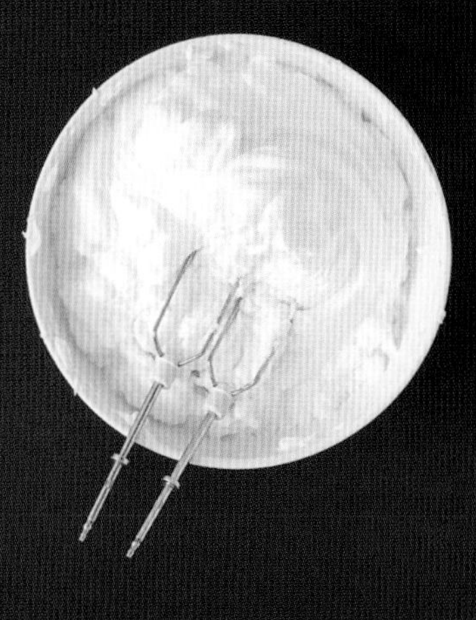

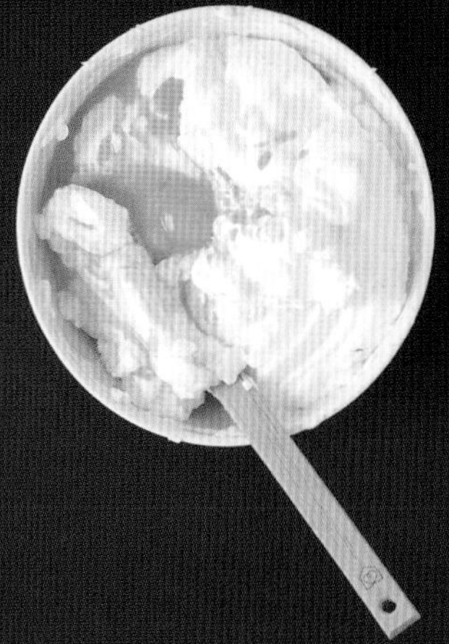

1 2

3 4

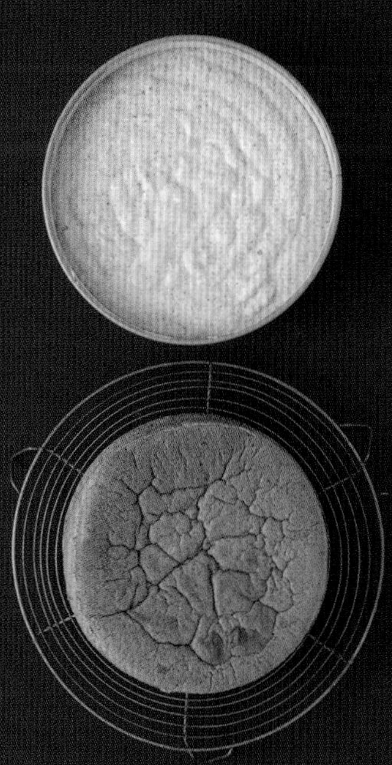

1	To prepare the ground walnut cake, separate the egg whites from the yolks, then whisk the 8 egg whites with an electric mixer until stiff, adding the sugar near the end.	2	Carefully fold in the egg yolks using a spatula.	
3	Sift the flour and ground walnuts together, then fold into the egg mixture	4	Butter and flour a round baking pan. Pour the batter into the pan and bake in a 340°F (170°C) oven for 30 minutes. Turn the cake out of the hot pan and set aside.	➢

5	To make the chopped walnut cake, whisk the 6 egg whites with an electric mixer until stiff, adding the sugar near the end.	6	Sift the flour, then gradually fold it to the egg whites using a spatula.
7	Fold in the chopped nuts.	8	Pour into the same pan used earlier, again buttered and floured. Bake for 20 minutes. Turn the cake out of the hot pan and leave to cool.

9	To make the chocolate cream, melt the chocolate in a microwave oven or double boiler.	10	Whisk in the egg yolks, then allow to cool.	
11	Whip the butter and confectioners' sugar with an electric mixer until creamy.	12	Add the chocolate to the butter mixture and whip until the cream is uniform. Set aside.	➢

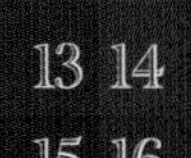

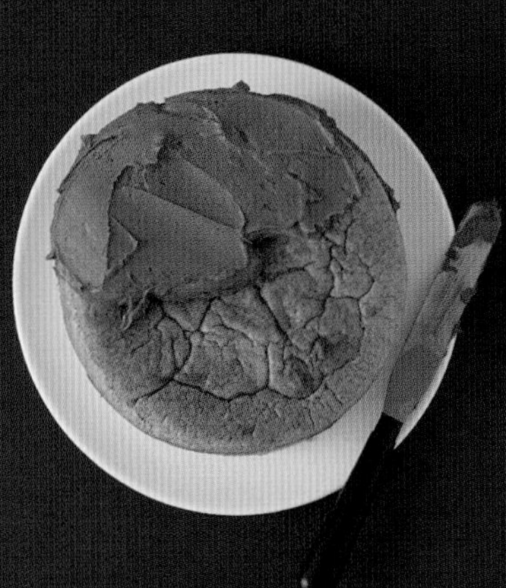

13	Slice the chopped walnut cake in half, creating two layers.	14	Place on a dish and soak the sliced surface with syrup. Next apply a layer of chocolate cream, about ¼ inch (0.5 cm) thick.
15	Place the entire ground walnut cake on top. Generously soak with syrup and spread a layer of chocolate cream on top.	16	Soak the sliced side of the other half of the chopped walnut cake. Place it on top, sliced side down. Soak the top with syrup and ice the top and sides with chocolate cream.

17	Refrigerate the cake for at least 1 hour.	**TIP** ☛ Serve in thin slices.

CHIC AND PRECIOUS

6

BOX OF CHOCOLATES

YIELD: ABOUT 2 POUNDS (1 KG) • PREPARATION: 2½ HOURS • COOKING: 50 MINUTES

FOR THE WHITE TRUFFLES:
7 ounces (200 g) white chocolate
3 ounces (80 g) pistachios (about ⅔ cup/150 ml)
2 tablespoons (30 ml) butter, softened
1 tablespoon (15 ml) confectioners' sugar
1 to 1½ tablespoons (15 to 22 ml) matcha
7 tablespoons (105 ml) heavy cream (36%)

FOR THE CHOCOLATE TRUFFLES:
⅞ cup (200 ml) heavy cream (36%)
7 ounces (200 g) dark chocolate
2 tablespoons (30 ml) butter
7 tablespoon (105 ml) cocoa powder

FOR THE FUDGE:
3½ ounces (100 g) nougat
6 ounces (175 g) dark chocolate
⅔ cup (150 ml) sweetened condensed milk
Pinch salt
1¾ ounces (50 g) pistachios (about ½ cup/125 ml)
1 tablespoon (15 ml) butter

FOR THE ROCHER PRALINES:
1 vanilla bean
⅔ cup (150 ml) sugar
10 ounces (280 g) hazelnuts
10 ounces (280 g) milk chocolate
1 ounce (20 g) dark chocolate

FOR THE FLORENTINES:
1¾ ounces (50 g) dark chocolate
3 ounces (80 g) dried fruit
7 strips candied orange peel

WHITE TRUFFLES (YIELD: ABOUT 30 TRUFFLES)			
1	Melt the white chocolate in a double boiler or microwave oven. Chop the pistachios.	2	Work the butter with the confectioners' sugar, then add the melted white chocolate and half of the matcha. Mix.
3	Whip the cream with an electric mixer until stiff and then carefully fold into the chocolate mixture. Allow to set in the refrigerator for about 30 minutes.	4	Mix the remaining matcha and the pistachios. Form balls of the chilled white chocolate mixture using your hands. Roll in the pistachio-matcha mixture. Refrigerate.

1 2
3 4

CHOCOLATE TRUFFLES (YIELD: ABOUT 30 TRUFFLES)			
1	Prepare a ganache using the cream and dark chocolate (see recipe 8).	2	Once the ganache is smooth, add the butter in 3 batches. Set aside in the refrigerator for 3 hours.
3	Using a spoon, remove small amounts of ganache and form balls using your hands.	4	Roll the balls in the cocoa to coat. Remove the excess cocoa by shaking the truffles in a strainer. Set aside in the refrigerator.

1 2
3 4

FUDGE (YIELD: ABOUT 20 SQUARES)

1	Slice the nougat into small pieces.	2	In a saucepan, melt the chocolate with the sweetened condensed milk, butter and salt.
3	Once the mixture is uniform, add the nougat and pistachios.	4	Pour into a rectangular pan and allow to set in the refrigerator before cutting into squares.

1 2

3 4

ROCHER PRALINES (YIELD: ABOUT 15 ROCHERS)			
1	Prepare the hazelnut praline paste (see recipe 10) using the vanilla, sugar and 5 ounces (150 g) whole hazelnuts.	2	Melt 3 ounces (80 g) milk chocolate and the dark chocolate in a microwave oven. Mix into the praline paste. Refrigerate for 30 minutes.
3	Using a spoon, scoop out a little chocolate praline paste and put a whole hazelnut in the center.	4	Roll between your hands to form a little ball. Set aside in the refrigerator for at least 2 hours.

5 6
7 8

5	Chop 1¾ ounces (50 g) whole hazelnuts.	6	Roll the rocchers in the chopped hazelnuts.
7	Melt 7 ounces (200 g) milk chocolate in a double boiler. Dip the rochers in the chocolate to coat.	8	Allow the chocolates to harden in the refrigerator.

1 2
3 4

FLORENTINES (YIELD: ABOUT 15)

1	Melt two-thirds of the chocolate in a double boiler or microwave oven. Add the remaining third and mix until completely melted.	2	Place a small teaspoon of melted chocolate on a silicone sheet or piece of waxed paper or parchment paper.
3	Using the back of the spoon, flatten to form a 1½- to 2-inch (4 to 5 cm) disk. Arrange 3 pieces of dried fruit and half a strip of candied orange peel on each florentine.	4	Set aside at room temperature. Once cooled, the florentines are easy to remove from the paper.

SUGGESTION FOR CHOCOLATE TRUFFLES	FUDGE VARIATION
☛ Chocolate truffles can be flavored using an alcohol of your choice, such as rum, cognac or whiskey.	Marshmallows and walnuts, pieces of caramel and hazelnuts and the like can be substituted for the pistachios and nougat. **FLORENTINES VARIATION** The florentines can also be made using milk chocolate or white chocolate.

63

CHOCOLATE-CHESTNUT SQUARES

⇝ YIELD: 12 SERVINGS • PREPARATION: 45 MINUTES • BAKING: 25 MINUTES • RESTING: 2½ HOURS ⇜

1 genoise, prepared and baked (see recipe 4)

FOR THE SYRUP:

¼ cup (60 ml) sugar
7 tablespoons (105 ml) water
2 tablespoons (30 ml) whiskey (optional)

FOR THE CHESTNUT CREAM:

5½ ounces (160 g) vacuum-packed chestnuts
1 pound (450 g) canned chestnut puree
6½ tablespoons (97 ml) butter, softened
⅔ cup (150 ml) heavy cream (36%)
1 tablespoon (15 ml) vanilla extract
4 large chestnuts in syrup or glazed chestnuts

FOR THE ICING:

⅔ cup (150 ml) heavy cream (36%), heated
5 ounces (150 g) dark chocolate morsels (about ¾ cup/175 ml)

1 2
3 4

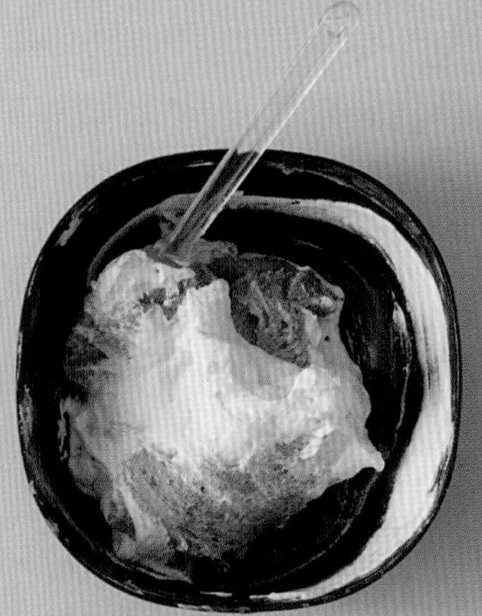

1	Melt the sugar in the water, then remove from the heat and add the whiskey. Set aside.	2	Blend the vacuum-packed chestnuts and chestnut puree in a blender or food processor.
3	Whisk the blended chestnuts into the butter.	4	With an electric mixer, whip ⅔ cup (150 ml) cream with the vanilla until stiff, then carefully fold into the chestnut mixture to create a chestnut cream. ➢

5	Line a plastic container with plastic wrap and spread a thin layer of chestnut cream into the bottom of the container. Cut 3 squares in the genoise that are slightly smaller than the container.	6	Place one square of genoise in the container, press down lightly and soak with syrup. Spread a second layer of cream, making it thicker and allowing it to flow over the sides of the genoise. Arrange the pieces of chestnut in syrup on top of the cream and press down lightly.
7	Add the second piece of genoise, and another layer of cream and chestnut pieces. Finish with the last square of genoise. Seal the container and allow to set in the refrigerator for at least 2 hours.	8	Prepare the icing (see recipe 8) by pouring the hot cream over the chocolate morsels.

9	Turn the cake out onto a rack. Place the rack over a large plate. Pour the icing over the cake and smooth with a spatula, letting the excess icing drip onto the plate. Refrigerate until the chocolate hardens a little.	**TIP** ☛ During the holidays, this cake can be prepared up to 2 days in advance, which will make it taste even better. Leave the cake in the container and ice it in the morning to serve that evening. **TIP** ☛ The excess icing can be used to decorate truffles.

CARL'S ROUNDS

YIELD: 8 SERVINGS • PREPARATION: 30 MINUTES • BAKING: 15 MINUTES • RESTING: 4 HOURS

FOR THE QUENELLES:

⅔ cup (150 ml) heavy cream (36%)
⅔ cup (150 ml) milk
3 tablespoons (45 ml) sugar
3 egg yolks
6 ounces (170 g) dark chocolate morsels (⅞ cup/200 ml)

FOR THE CRUST:

1 ounces (30 g) milk chocolate morsels (about 2½ tbsp/37 ml)
2 teaspoons (10 ml) butter
3 ounces (80 g) hazelnut praline paste (see recipe 10) or 3½ ounces (100 g) hazelnut-flavored milk chocolate
1½ cups (375 ml) puffed rice cereal

1 2

3 4

1	Bring the cream and milk to a boil in a saucepan.	2	Whisk the sugar and egg yolks.	
3	Make a crème anglaise by first pouring a little of the hot cream mixture into the egg mixture, then pouring the egg-cream mixture into the saucepan. Cook over low heat, stirring, until the mixture coats the spoon.	4	Pour the hot crème anglaise over the dark chocolate, set aside for 2 minutes then whisk until smooth. Allow to set in the refrigerator for at least 4 hours, overnight if possible.	➢

5 6

7 8

5	Melt the milk chocolate and butter in a double boiler, then mix in the praline paste (or melt the hazelnut-flavored milk chocolate in a microwave oven).	6	Add the puffed rice to the chocolate mixture and mix. Set aside, at room temperature.
7	When ready to serve, create a small round with the puffed rice mixture on each plate, using a cookie cutter or a small can that is open at both ends.	8	Using 2 identical spoons, form a small quenelle of chocolate cream and place on the round.

9	It's ready!	**OPTION** ❊ Heat 1 cup (250 ml) milk with ½ teaspoon (2 ml) vanilla extract. Blend until foamy, as for a cappuccino. Scoop the foam with a spoon and drop around the rounds. Serve immediately.

CHOCOLATE MACAROONS

YIELD: 20 MACAROONS • PREPARATION: 45 MINUTES • BAKING: 20 MINUTES • RESTING: 1 NIGHT

FOR THE GANACHE FILLING:
⅞ cup (200 ml) heavy cream (36%)
6½ ounces (180 g) dark chocolate
1 teaspoon (5 ml) coffee extract

FOR THE COOKIES:
1½ cups (375 ml) ground almonds
1¾ cups (375 ml) confectioners' sugar
3 tablespoons (45 ml) cocoa powder
4 egg whites, room temperature
⅓ cup (75 ml) superfine sugar

1 2

3 4

1	Prepare the ganache (see recipe 8), adding the coffee extract at the end. Cover the ganache by placing plastic wrap directly on top of it and set aside.	2	For plain macaroons, use a 2-inch (5 cm) diameter cookie cutter to trace circles on a piece of parchment paper. Line a baking sheet with the parchment paper and set aside.	
3	Sift together the ground almonds, the confectioners' sugar and the cocoa. Using a food processor, blend until a fine powder is obtained.	4	Using an electric mixer, whisk the whites until stiff, gradually adding the superfine sugar.	➢

5 6
7 8

5	Add the almond mixture and fold in. The whites should fall a little. Continue folding for 2 minutes: the dough should be smooth, shiny and supple.	6	Fill a pastry bag fitted with a ½-inch (1 cm) tip with dough. Pipe dough on the circles on the parchment paper and let harden at room temperature for 30 minutes.
7	Bake for 20 minutes. If these are small macaroons, reduce the baking time to 15 minutes. Leave to cool.	8	Turn the macaroons over and spread ganache on every other one.

9	Sandwich the cookies and refrigerate overnight. Before serving the next day, allow to warm up to room temperature, about 30 minutes.	**STORAGE** Macaroons freeze well. You can freeze the cookie portions and fill them later, or freeze the filled cookies in an airtight container. Take them out 1 hour prior to serving.

EASY MACAROONS

YIELD: 8 MACAROONS • PREPARATION: 20 MINUTES • BAKING: 20 MINUTES • RESTING: 30 MINUTES

FOR THE GANACHE:
7 tablespoons (105 ml) heavy cream (36%)
3 ounces (90 g) dark chocolate

FOR THE DOUGH:
2½ tablespoons (37 ml) flour
¼ cup (60 ml) + ⅓ cup (75 ml) superfine sugar
7½ tablespoons (112 ml) ground almonds
2 egg whites
2 tablespoons (30 ml) confectioners' sugar

PRELIMINARY:
Draw 2-inch (5 cm) diameter circles on a piece of parchment paper. Preheat the oven to 350°F (180°C).

1 2

3 4

1	Prepare a ganache (see recipe 8) using the cream and chocolate.	2	Prepare the dough as described in recipe 65. Mix the flour, confectioners' sugar and almond powder then whisk the egg whites and superfine sugar, and then fold the dry mixture into the egg whites.
3	Fill a pastry bag fitted with a 1-inch (2.5 cm) tip with dough. Pipe dough on the circles on the parchment paper and bake for 20 minutes. Let cool. Dust with confectioners' sugar.	4	Turn the macaroons over and spread ganache on every other one. Place each macaroon without ganache on top of a macaroon with ganache. Chill the macaroons in the refrigerator for 30 minutes before serving.

MATCHA LAYER CAKE

YIELD: 8 TO 10 SERVINGS • PREPARATION: 50 MINUTES • BAKING: 15 MINUTES • RESTING: 2 HOURS

FOR THE CAKE:
1¾ cups (375 ml) ground almonds
4 eggs + 4 egg whites
1⅛ cup (280 ml) confectioners' sugar
⅓ cup (75 ml) flour
1 to 1½ tablespoons (15 to 22 ml) matcha
1 tablespoon (15 ml) superfine sugar
2½ tablespoons (37 ml) butter, melted and cooled
2 ounces (60 g) dark chocolate

FOR THE BUTTERCREAM:
1⅔ cups (300 ml) water
6 tablespoons (90 ml) superfine sugar
3 egg yolks, room temperature
1 to 1½ tablespoons (15 to 22 ml) matcha
⅔ cup (150 ml) butter, softened

FOR THE GANACHE:
7 ounces dark chocolate
3 tablespoons (45 ml) butter, softened
7 tablespoons (105 ml) milk
3½ tablespoons (52 ml) heavy cream (36%)

FOR THE SYRUP:
1 vanilla bean
½ cup (125 ml) superfine sugar

1 2
3 4

1	For the ganache, coarsely chop the dark chocolate, cut the softened butter into pieces and add to the chocolate.	2	Bring the milk and cream to a boil, then pour this mixture over the chocolate-butter mixture (see recipe 8).	
3	Mix until it forms a smooth ganache.	4	To make the syrup, halve the vanilla bean and scrape out the seeds. Heat the superfine sugar with the vanilla seeds and scraped vanilla bean in ⅞ cup (200 ml) water. Once the sugar melts, remove the bean and set aside.	➢

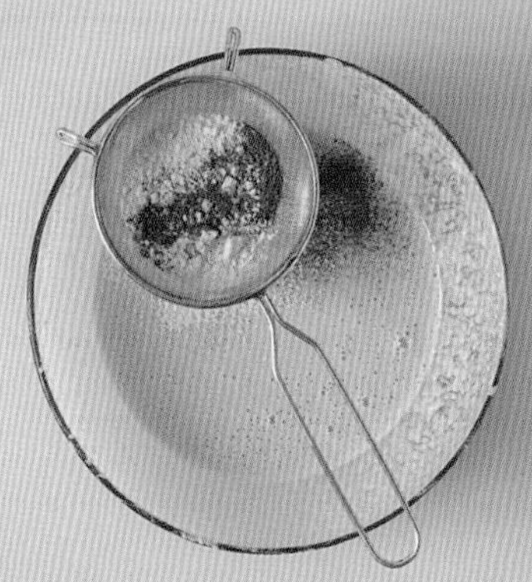

5 6
7 8

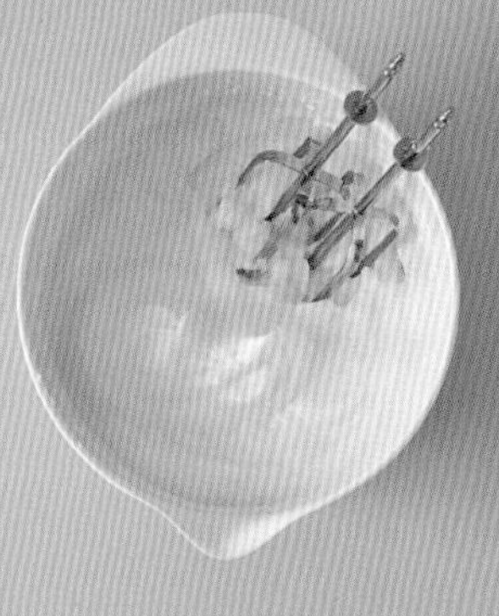

5	To make the cake, beat the 4 whole eggs with the ground almonds and confectioners' sugar with an electric mixer. The mixture should double in volume (beat for about 3 minutes).	6	Sift the flour and matcha into the egg mixture and mix.
7	With an electric mixer, beat the egg whites with the superfine sugar until stiff.	8	Carefully fold the whites into the egg-matcha mixture and finish with the butter.

9 10
11 12

9	Spread the batter onto two baking sheets lined with parchment paper. Bake in a 425°F (220°C) oven for 8 minutes. Remove the cake layers from the paper when cooled. Cut in half widthwise.	10	Melt the 2 ounces (60 g) dark chocolate in a microwave oven. Spread the melted chocolate on one side of one cake layer and then refrigerate. Set aside the other three layers.	
11	Prepare the buttercream (see recipe 1): heat the water and sugar and cook for 5 minutes from the point at which the sugar melts.	12	With an electric mixer, whisk the egg yolks. Whisk in the melted sugar, then add the matcha and butter. The buttercream should be smooth and uniform.	➢

13 14
15 16

13	Remove the cake iced with chocolate from the refrigerator. Using a brush, generously soak the non-iced side with vanilla syrup.	14	Spread a layer of buttercream on top and smooth with a spatula.
15	Position a second cake layer on top of the buttercream, Soak generously with syrup and spread a layer of ganache on top.	16	Position a third cake layer on top, generously soak with syrup and spread a layer of ganache on top. Finish with the last cake layer and the remaining syrup and ganache.

17	Set aside in the refrigerator for at least 2 hours. Before serving, trim the sides using a hot knife.	**THE DIFFERENT LAYERS** In all, there should be four layers of well-soaked cake, two layers of buttercream and two layers of ganache: cake, buttercream, cake, ganache, cake, buttercream, cake, ganache.

CHOCOLATE-RASPBERRY LOAF

YIELD: 8 SERVINGS • PREPARATION: 40 MINUTES • BAKING: 20 MINUTES • RESTING: 2 HOURS

FOR THE SPONGE CAKE:
6 eggs
⅔ cup (150 ml) sugar
3 tablespoons (45 ml) cocoa powder
½ cup (125 ml) ground almonds

FOR THE SYRUP:
¼ cup (60 ml) sugar
2 teaspoons (10 ml) raspberry liqueur

FOR THE GANACHE:
1½ cups (375 ml) heavy cream (36%)
1 vanilla bean
12½ ounces (350 g) dark chocolate
7 ounces (200 g) raspberries

PRELIMINARY:
Preheat the oven to 350°F (180°C).
Separate the egg whites from the yolks.

1

2

3

4

5

6

1	With an electric mixer, beat the egg yolks with 1½ tablespoons (22 ml) sugar until the mixture becomes pale.	2	Whisk the whites with an electric mixer until stiff, gradually whisking in the remaining sugar.	3	Carefully fold the yolk mixture into the whites mixture.	
4	Fold in the cocoa and ground almonds.	5	Pour into a buttered and floured baking pan. Bake for 20 minutes.	6	Let cool, then cut the cake into 4 equal pieces widthwise.	➢

7 8
9 10

7	To make the syrup, bring 7 tablespoons (105 ml) water and the sugar to a boil. As soon as the sugar melts, remove from the heat and add the liqueur. Set aside.	8	Prepare the ganache (see recipe 8), adding the seeds from the vanilla bean to the cream once it's boiled. Divide the ganache in half.
9	Line a loaf pan with plastic wrap. Put a layer of cake, cut side facing up, into the pan. Soak with syrup. Spread ganache and arrange half of the raspberries on top.	10	Cover the berries with ganache and place another layer of sponge cake on top. Soak with syrup and add another layer of ganache and berries. End with the last layer of sponge cake, which will serve as the base of the cake loaf.

11 Turn the sponge cake out onto a rack, over a plate. Reheat the second half of the ganache in a double boiler or microwave oven. Pour the ganache uniformly over the sponge cake and smooth using a spatula, catching any drips on the plate. Refrigerate until ready to serve.

TIPS

☛ The cake loaf will taste better if you prepare it in the morning for that evening or, better still, the day before for the next day.

☛ A genoise (see recipe 4) can be substituted for the sponge cake.

HAZELNUT DACQUOISE

YIELD: 8 SERVINGS • PREPARATION: 40 MINUTES • BAKING: 30 MINUTES • RESTING: 2 HOURS

FOR THE MERINGUES:
6 egg whites
¾ cup (175 ml) sugar
1½ ounces (40 g) almonds, ground
2 ounces (60 g) hazelnuts, ground
2½ ounces (70 g) whole hazelnuts

FOR THE FILLING:
¼ cup (60 ml) sugar
1 tablespoon (15 ml) cornstarch
2 egg yolks
1 cup (250 ml) milk
3½ ounces (100 g) dark chocolate, chopped
⅞ cup (210 ml) butter, softened
3 ounces (80 g) hazelnut praline paste (see recipe 10)

PRELIMINARY:
On two pieces of parchment paper, draw two 9-inch (23 cm) diameter circles. Line two baking sheets with the parchment paper and set aside.

1	With an electric mixer, beat the egg whites, gradually adding the sugar.	2	Once the mixture is stiff and shiny, carefully fold in the ground almonds and ground hazelnuts using a spatula.	
3	Pour the meringue mixture onto the circle outlines and spread to an even thickness with a spatula. Coarsely chop the whole hazelnuts and sprinkle on top of the meringues.	4	Bake in a 350°F (180°C) oven for 30 minutes.	➢

5	Prepare the pastry cream for the filling (see recipe 3) using the sugar, cornstarch, egg yolks and milk. Remove from the heat, then add the chocolate. Whisk to combine.	6	Work the softened butter with the whisk, then add the praline paste.
7	Whisk the butter mixture into the cooled chocolate pastry cream to make a nice mousseline filling.	8	Place the mousseline in a pastry bag fitted with a ⅝-inch (1.5 cm) tip and decorate one meringue disk, forming balls.

9	Cover with the other disk. Refrigerate for at least 2 hours before serving.	**TIP** ☛ A bar of hazelnut-flavored milk chocolate can be substituted for the dark chocolate and hazelnut praline paste. Add the milk chocolate to the pastry cream when it's still hot, and reduce the amount of sugar in the pastry cream to 1 tablespoon (15 ml).

CAPPUCCINO PIE

YIELD: 8 SERVINGS • PREPARATION: 40 MINUTES • BAKING: 25 MINUTES • RESTING: 1 HOUR, 15 MINUTES

FOR THE SUGAR PASTRY:
⅔ cup (150 ml) butter
½ cup (125 ml) sugar
1 egg
1⅔ cups (400 ml) flour
1½ tablespoons (22 ml) cocoa powder
½ cup (125 ml) ground almonds
1 teaspoon (5 ml) vanilla extract

FOR THE COFFEE GANACHE:
1½ cups (375 ml) heavy cream (36%)
1 teaspoon (5 ml) instant coffee
9 ounces (250 g) dark chocolate

FOR THE MASCARPONE CREAM:
2 sugar cubes or 2 teaspoons granulated sugar
1 very short espresso or 1 teaspoon instant coffee in 3½ tablespoons (52 ml) water
9 ounces (250 g) mascarpone (about 1 cup/250 ml)

PRELIMINARY:
Preheat the oven to 350°F (180°C).

1 2

3 4

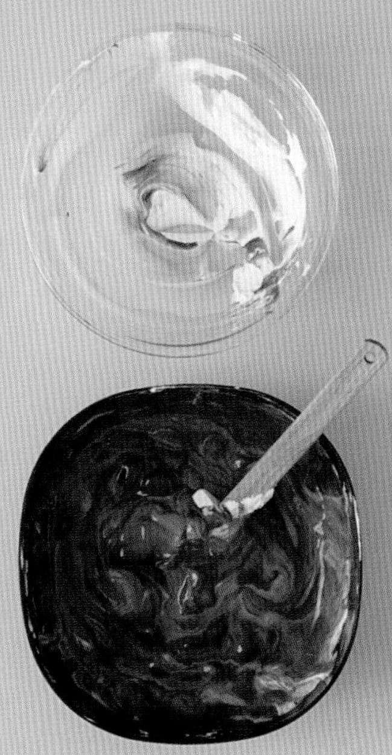

1	Prepare the sugar pastry (see recipe 5), adding the cocoa with the flour. Wrap the dough in plastic wrap and allow to rest and harden in the refrigerator.	2	To make the ganache, bring about ⅞ cup (200 ml) heavy cream and the instant coffee to a boil. Pour the hot cream mixture over the chocolate. Set aside for 2 minutes.	
3	Whisk the cream mixture and the chocolate together, making large circles from the center out. Let cool.	4	With an electric mixer, whip ⅔ cup (150 ml) heavy cream until stiff then fold into the warm ganache. Set aside in the refrigerator.	➢

5 6

7 8

5	Roll out the chilled sugar pastry dough on a floured work surface, then roll it into a buttered non-stick baking pan. Prick the bottom with a fork and freeze for 15 minutes.	6	Line the dough with parchment paper, fill with pie weights or dried beans and bake for 20 minutes. Turn out of the pan and let cool on a rack.
7	To make the mascarpone cream, first dissolve the sugar in the espresso. Whisk the sweetened espresso into the mascarpone. Spread onto the cooled piecrust.	8	Fill a pastry bag fitted with a fluted tip with ganache and pipe small rosettes onto the mascarpone cream.

9	Keep the pie in the refrigerator until ready to serve.	**TIPS** ☛ Refrigerate the dough before baking it. The colder the dough is, the better the sides will hold while it bakes. ☛ Use a knife to mark squares on the cream layer, as a guide, so you can pipe the right number of rosettes.

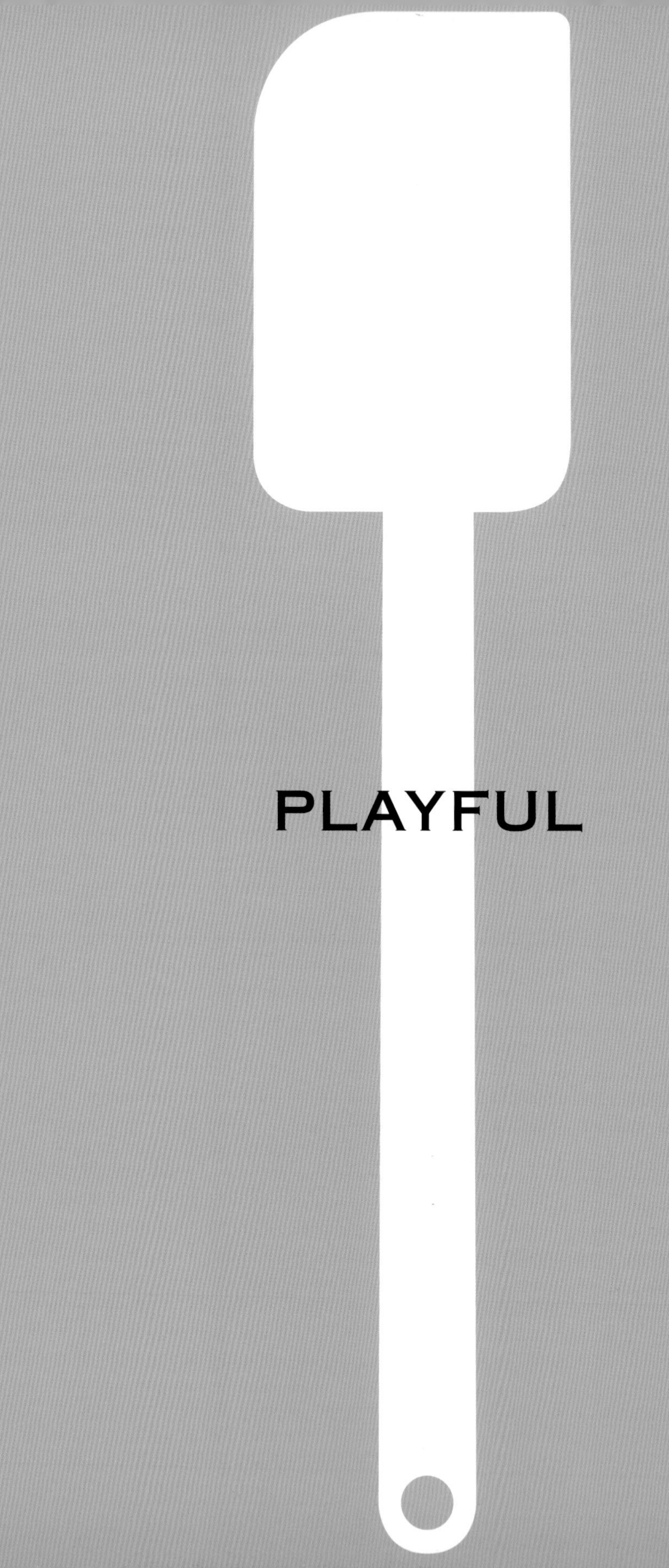

PLAYFUL

7

71

COCONUT BARS

YIELD: 10 BARS (1 OUNCE/30 G EACH) • PREPARATION: 15 MINUTES • RESTING: 2½ HOURS

⅔ cup (150 ml) sweetened condensed milk
1½ cups (375 ml) shredded coconut
7 ounces (200 g) milk chocolate
¼ cup (60 ml) canola or grapeseed oil

NOTE:
The coating can be made without oil, which will make it thicker and harder.

1 2

3 4

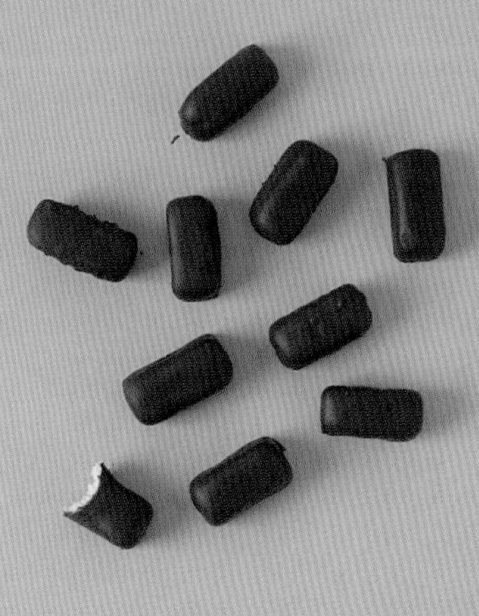

1	Mix the condensed milk and coconut.	2	Shape into bite-sized bars and place them on a piece of parchment paper. Freeze for 2 hours.
3	Melt the chocolate and oil in a microwave oven. Using a fork, dip the bars in chocolate to coat.	4	Refrigerate for about 30 minutes. The bars are ready when the chocolate coating hardens.

CHOCOLATE SANDWICH COOKIES

YIELD: 8 COOKIES • PREPARATION: 40 MINUTES • BAKING: 15 MINUTES • RESTING: 1 HOUR, 15 MINUTES

½ cup (125 ml) butter, softened
⅔ cup (150 ml) confectioners' sugar
Pinch of salt
1 egg + 1 yolk

1⅔ cups (400 ml) flour
½ cup (125 ml) ground almonds
Chocolate-hazelnut spread (see recipe 11), for the filling

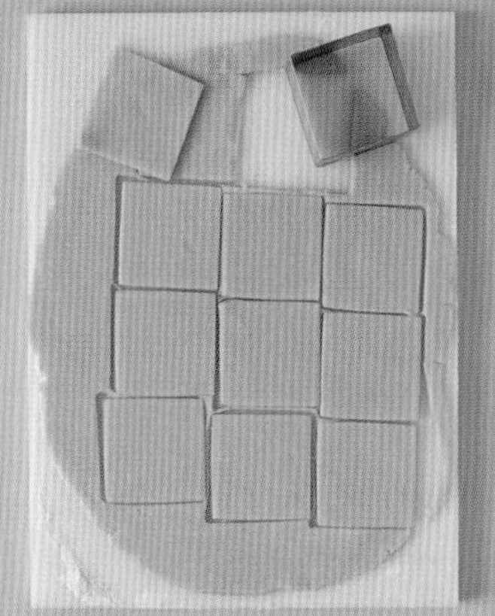

1 2 3

4 5 6

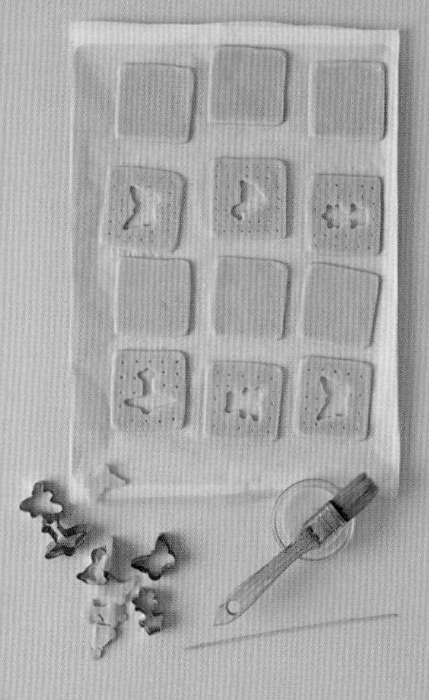

1	Whisk the softened butter with the confectioners' sugar and salt, and then add the egg.	2	Mix in the flour and almonds until the mixture forms a ball. Refrigerate for about 1 hour.	3	Roll out the dough to a thickness of ⅛ inch (3 mm). Cut out an even number of squares using a cookie cutter.
4	Cut out the center of half of the squares using a smaller cookie cutter. Whisk the egg yolk with a little milk or water and brush the squares with the cutout with the egg wash.	5	Bake for 15 minutes at 340°F (170°C). Let cool.	6	Completely coat the shortbread cookies without cutouts with the spread. Position the shortbreads with cutouts on top. Refrigerate for 15 minutes.

73

BUTTER-COOKIE CAKE

YIELD: 8 SERVINGS • PREPARATION: 20 MINUTES • RESTING: 1 HOUR

1 tablespoon (15 ml) granulated sugar
½ cup (125 ml) coffee
5 ounces (150 g) dark chocolate
⅞ cup (210 ml) butter, softened
¾ cup (175 ml) confectioners' sugar
24 butter cookies (Petit Beurre cookies work best)

PRELIMINARY:
Mix the granulated sugar into the coffee.

1 2 3

4 5 6

1	Melt the chocolate in a microwave oven.	2	Mix the softened butter and the confectioners' sugar.	3	Whisk the melted chocolate into the butter mixture until uniform.
4	Arrange 6 cookies on a square platter. Soak the cookies with coffee.	5	Cover with a layer of chocolate cream, and then arrange a second row of cookies on top. Repeat 3 times.	6	Smooth the sides and the top of the cake with the rest of the cream. Refrigerate for at least 1 hour.

CHOCOLATE BUNS

YIELD: 8 BUNS • PREPARATION: 30 MINUTES • RESTING: 1 HOUR, 15 MINUTES • BAKING: 20 MINUTES

7 tablespoons (105 ml) milk
¼ ounce (7 g) yeast
3½ ounces (100 g) chocolate-hazelnut spread (see recipe 11) or 8 milk chocolate square

2 cups (500 ml) flour
½ teaspoon (2 ml) salt
¼ cup (60 ml) sugar
2 eggs
¼ cup (60 ml) butter, softened and diced

PRELIMINARY:
Warm the milk in a microwave oven and mix the yeast in the milk. Preheat the oven to 105°F (40°C), or its lowest temperature setting.

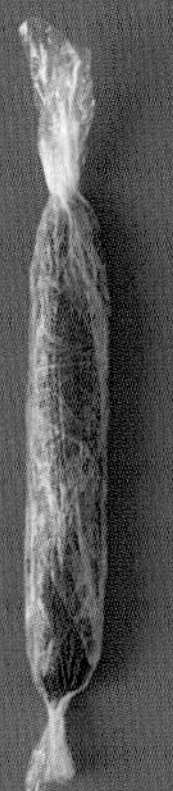

1 2

3 4

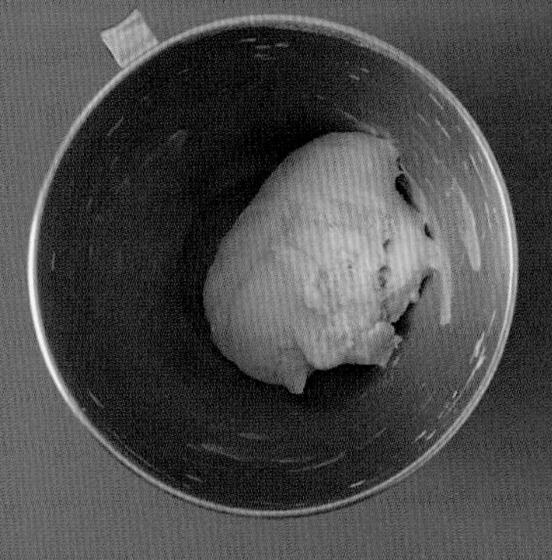

1	Pour the spread onto a sheet of plastic wrap and roll to form a sausage shape. Set aside in the freezer.	2	Sift the flour, then add the salt, sugar, 1 egg and the milk-yeast mixture.
3	Knead in an electric mixer fitted with a dough hook for about 10 minutes, until the dough forms a ball that does not stick to the side.	4	Add the butter and knead until completely incorporated: the dough must be smooth and supple. Turn the oven off and leave the dough in it to rise for 30 minutes. ➢

5 6

7 8

5	Punch down the dough and fold over; cover with a dish towel and let rest in the refrigerator for 15 minutes.	6	Preheat the oven again to 105°F (40°C), or the lowest temperature. Shape the dough into 8 small buns.
7	Slice the hardened spread into 8 sections and put a piece of spread or a square of milk chocolate in the center of each bun.	8	Put the buns in a baking pan. Turn off the oven, cover the buns and let rest in the oven for 30 minutes. Whisk 1 egg with a little water or milk and brush the risen buns with the egg wash.

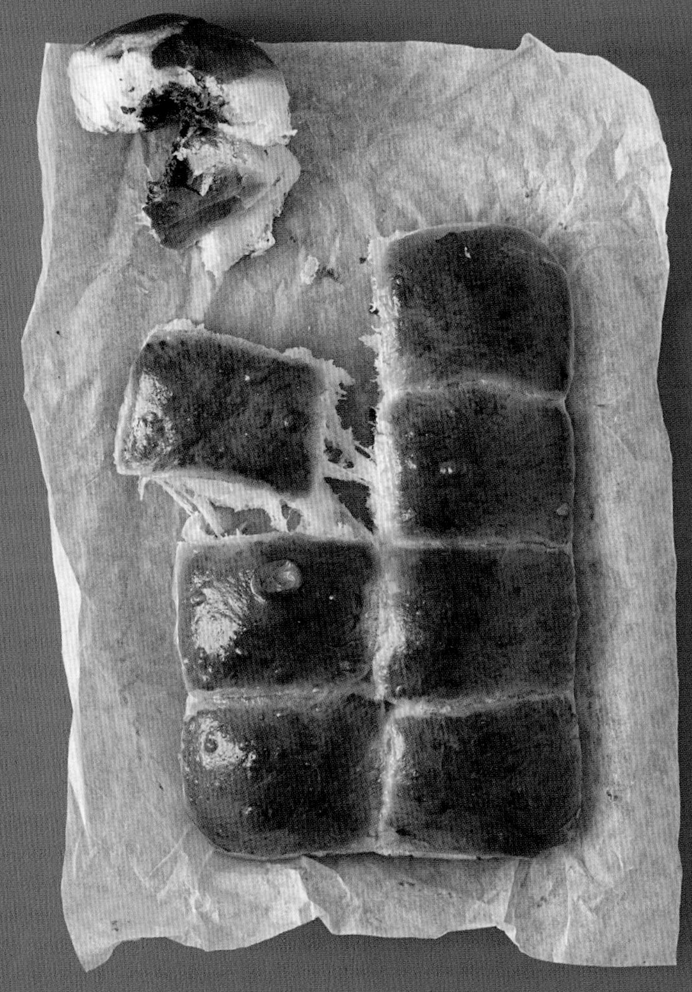

9	Bake in a 350°F (180°C) oven for 20 minutes. Serve warm.

TIP

☛ These buns can be shaped however you wish. Bake them on a baking sheet lined with a piece of parchment paper.

VARIATION

The buns can be filled with leftover ganache or dark, milk or white chocolate morsels. Follow the same method described in step 7.

CHOCOLATE SHORTBREAD PUZZLES

YIELD: TWO 4-PIECE PUZZLES • PREPARATION: 20 MINUTES • RESTING: 1 HOUR • BAKING: 12 MINUTES

2 cups (500 ml) flour
3 tablespoons (45 ml) cocoa
⅔ cup (150 ml) butter, softened

⅔ cup (150 ml) sugar
1 egg
Pinch salt

PRELIMINARY:
Sift the flour and cocoa together.

1 2
3 4

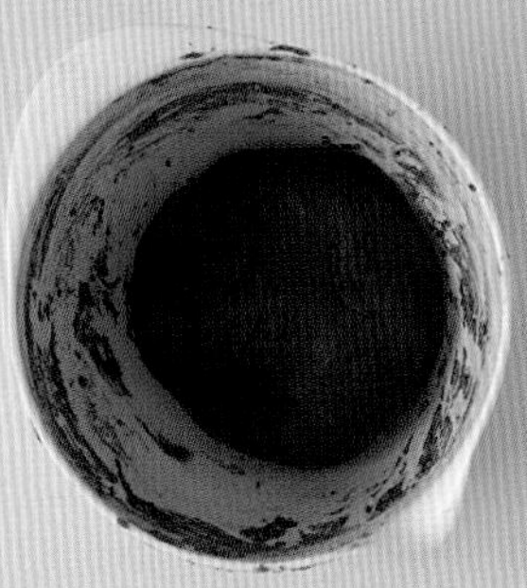

1	Mix the softened butter and the sugar.	2	Mix in the egg.	
3	Mix in the flour mixture.	4	Mix until the dough forms a uniform ball. Do not overwork the dough, as it will lose its elasticity.	➢

5 6
7 8

5	Divide the dough in half. Cover both dough balls with plastic wrap and let rest and harden in the refrigerator.	6	Roll out one of the dough balls into a ¼-inch (0.5 cm) thick rectangle. Trim the rectangle with a knife to neaten the edges and round off the corners with your fingers.
7	Using the tip of the knife, trace, without cutting, 4 puzzle pieces.	8	Bake on a baking sheet in a 340°F (170°C) oven for 12 minutes. Take the shortbreads out of the oven and cut out the puzzle pieces by following the guidelines.

9	Allow the shortbreads to cool before trying to separate the pieces.	**TIP** ☛ Save the second half of the dough to create a second puzzle or lollipop cookies (see recipe 77).

CHOCOLATE LOLLIPOPS

YIELD: 8 LOLLIPOPS • PREPARATION: 10 MINUTES • RESTING: 1 HOUR

3½ ounces (100 g) milk chocolate
¼ cup (60 ml) heavy cream (36%)
Walnut pieces

Colored sprinkles
Colored decorations

PRELIMINARY:
Coarsely chop the chocolate

76

1 2

3 4

1	Prepare a ganache using the cream and the chocolate (see recipe 8).	2	Place different decorations (sprinkles, colored beads, confetti, crushed walnuts and the like) into a silicone lollipop mold.
3	Pour the ganache into the individual mold cups, then cover with the different decorations.	4	Freeze for 2 hours. Unmold the lollipops, insert a skewer into each and serve as soon as possible.

77

COOKIE LOLLIPOPS

YIELD: 8 LOLLIPOPS • PREPARATION: 15 MINUTES • BAKING: 15 MINUTES

½ batch chocolate shortbread puzzle dough (see recipe 75) or:
1⅓ cups (325 ml) flour
¼ cup (60 ml) butter, softened
⅓ cup (75 ml) sugar
1 egg
1½ tablespoons (22 ml) cocoa powder
Pinch of salt
Colored sprinkles

PRELIMINARY:
Prepare the dough (see recipe 75).

1 2

3 4

1	Form 1-inch (2 cm) diameter dough balls and flatten them by crushing them with the palm of your hand — maintain a thickness of ½ inch (1 cm).	2	Insert a skewer or stick into the side of each flattened ball.
3	Place one side of each cookie on a plate with decorations, pressing lightly to make them stick to the dough.	4	Arrange the lollipops on a non-stick baking sheet (or a baking sheet lined with parchment paper) and bake in a 340°F (170°C) oven for 15 minutes.

CHOCOLATE MARSHMALLOW LOLLIPOPS

YIELD: 15 LOLLILOPS • PREPARATION: 40 MINUTES • BAKING: 10 MINUTES • RESTING: 2½ HOURS

⅓ ounce (10½ g) unflavored gelatin powder or 6 sheets gelatin
1⅓ cups (325 ml) sugar
½ tablespoons (7 ml) honey
3 egg whites

1 tablespoon (15 ml) vanilla extract
7 ounces (200 g) milk chocolate morsels (about 1 cup/250 ml)
2 tablespoon (30 ml) canola or grapeseed oil

PRELIMINARY:
Dissolve the gelatin in a little cold water (if using sheet gelatin, soak in cold water until softened, then drain).

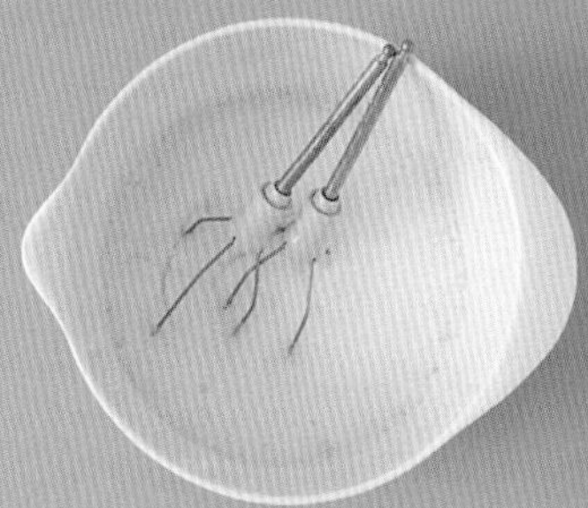

1 2

3 4

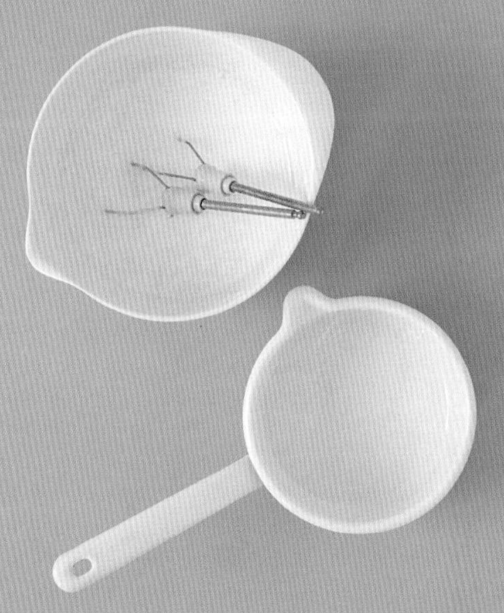

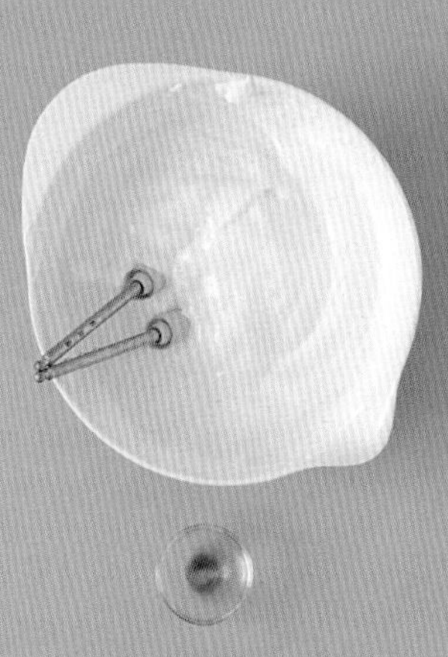

1	Over medium heat, cook 3⅓ cups (800 ml) water, the sugar and the honey until it reaches 266°F (130°C), about 8 to 10 minutes.	2	With an electric mixer, whisk the egg whites until foamy and semi-stiff.	
3	Pour the syrup in a thin stream over the egg whites while continuing to whisk.	4	Add the vanilla, then the gelatin, all while continuing to whisk. Whisk for 5 minutes, until the mixture is thick and warm.	➢

5 6

7 8

5	Pour into a pan or dish lined with parchment paper. Smooth the surface with a spatula and let set at room temperature for about 2 hours.	6	Remove the marshmallow rectangle from the dish. Using cookie cutters, cut out shapes, taking care to dip the cookie cutters in hot water between cuttings.
7	Arrange the marshmallow shapes on a piece of lightly oiled parchment paper. Insert a skewer into each marshmallow and let harden for 1 hour in the freezer.	8	Melt the chocolate and oil in a double boiler.

	Quickly dip the marshmallows in the chocolate. Allow the excess chocolate to drip back into the bowl by turning the skewer. Place on parchment paper and refrigerate until hard.	**VARIATION** Flavor the marshmallow using 3 tablespoons (45 ml) orange blossom water, 5 to 10 drops of rose water, mint, bergamot or citrus fruit zest.

79

TIERED CANDY CAKE

YIELD: 25 SERVINGS • PREPARATION: 2 HOURS

1 Styrofoam disk, 8 inches (20 cm) in diameter & 4 inches (10 cm) high
1 Styrofoam disk, 12 inches (30 cm) in diameter & 4 inches (10 cm) high

About 50 small macaroons (see recipe 65)
About 50 cookie lollipops (see recipe 77)
About 30 pinwheel cookies (see recipe 43)

One marshmallow lollipop shaped like a star (see recipe 78)

- Assemble the 2 disks by sticking 8 toothpicks into the top of the large round, then attach the small round by pushing down.
- You can cover the Styrofoam disks with black paper before attaching the cookies. This way, no white will show between the rows.
- Insert toothpicks into all the cookies, then attach them to the rounds in a regular pattern.
- Start with the sides of the large disk, attaching 2 rows of cookies.
- Continue on the sides of the small disk.
- Next decorate the top of the large disk.
- Finish with the top of the small disk, and crown with the marshmallow star.

APPENDIXES

GLOSSARY

TABLE OF CONTENTS

RECIPE INDEX

THEMATIC INDEX

ACKNOWLEDGMENTS

GLOSSARY

MARQUISE
A classic molded dessert that traditionally involves lining a mold with sponge cake, ladyfingers or buttered bread and filling with fruit, custard or whipped cream. The marquise is chilled overnight and unmolded before serving.

COCOA POWDER
Unsweetened cocoa powder is widely available in supermarkets and should not be confused with cocoa mix or instant cocoa. The latter are drink mixes and usually contain milk powder and sugar. Do not try to substitute cocoa mix or instant cocoa for cocoa powder.

CREAM
Only cream with a milk fat content of 30% or more can be whipped and will increase in volume, for whipped cream, ganache, mousses and the like. Unless the cream is being whipped, a lighter cream, such as light cream (20% milk fat) or table cream (18% milk fat), can often be substituted for heavy cream (36% milk fat).

CRÈME ANGLAISE
French for "English cream," a crème anglaise is a rich custard sauce. It can be poured over cakes, fruit and other desserts and can be flavored in any number of ways.

CRUMBLE
Crumble is a classic topping based on equal quantities of flour, butter and sugar. The ingredients are either rubbed together by hand or blended in a food processor until the mixture looks crumbly.

DACQUOISE
Traditionally based on almonds, this dessert can also be prepared with hazelnuts, pistachios or coconut. It consists of two layers of meringue with a layer of mousse, or other similarly airy filling, in between.

DOUBLE BOILER
A double boiler is a two-pan system, in which a saucepan or heatproof bowl is placed directly on top of a pan of simmering water. It provides a very gentle heat. Care must be taken to keep the top pan or bowl from touching the water, as that would provide too much heat. It is an ideal way to melt chocolate, although you can also heat chocolate in a microwave oven, in an appropriate container.

FLORENTINES
As the name implies, these candylike cookies have an Italian heritage. Usually made of a mixture of butter, sugar, cream, honey and candied fruit, they often have a chocolate coating on the bottom.

GANACHE
A traditional ganache is a mixture of melted chocolate and heavy cream. It can be thick (with more chocolate than cream) and used for truffles and to garnish cakes, or it can be sufficiently liquid to glaze a cake and be used as icing.

GENOISE
Originating in Genoa, a genoise is a light and fluffy cake made by beating eggs and sugar in a double boiler. It serves as a base for numerous filled cakes and as an accompaniment to creams and mousses.

HAZELNUT-FLAVORED MILK CHOCOLATE
Many different types of flavored chocolate can be found in supermarkets. Hazelnut is an excellent complement to milk and dark chocolate.

MADELEINES
These small spongy cakes are a classic French dessert and often eaten as cookies. They are baked in a special pan with scalloped cups, so the finished product is shaped like a shell.

MATCHA
Ground Japanese green tea.

MOLDS
Chocolate molds are available in a variety of materials (silicone, plastic, metal) and in a wide variety of shapes, for every holiday and any theme imaginable.

PANS
Non-stick silicone pans are easy to use. However, take care when moving them because they are soft and foods can spill out. Consider placing your silicone pan on a metal baking sheet before filling. Cake pans made of Pyrex, ceramic or metal (with or without a non-stick coating) need to be buttered and floured before use.

PANNA COTTA
Italian for "cooked cream," a panna cotta is a light custard dessert usually made with gelatin, giving it a slightly jiggly consistency. It is often served with fruit or a chocolate sauce.

PASTRY BAGS
You can use pastry bags made of plastic, for one-time use. They are cone shaped, and all that's required is cutting the bottom with a pair of scissors to insert the tip. Fill the bag with your mixture (cream or dough), shaking it a little, if necessary, to ensure there are no air bubbles. Lastly, close by twisting from the top down, until the mixture starts to come out of the tip. Based on the shape desired, choose either a fluted tip with teeth or a round tip to achieve a smooth effect. The size of the tip depends on the use. If a pastry bag is used without a tip, a smooth effect is obtained. A freezer bag cut at one corner can also serve as a pastry bag for simple decorations.

SACHERTORTE
Created by Viennese confectioner Franz Sacher in 1832, a Sachertorte is a rich chocolate layer cake filled with apricot jam. It is traditionally served with whipped cream.

SILICONE SHEET
A reusable and good-quality non-stick sheet. Unlike parchment paper, it doesn't crinkle when moistened. Can be found in supermarkets, department stores and cookware stores.

SOFTENED BUTTER
Softened butter is soft but not melted, so it can be worked easily with a spatula. It helps other ingredients blend together. Leave butter at room temperature to soften. Butter softens more quickly if it is cut into small pieces.

THICKENED CREAM
Thicken cream (such as for a crème anglaise) by heating it to 181°F (83°C), until it coats the back of a spoon. The cream must uniformly cover the spoon, and you should be able to trace a distinct furrow by running your finger along the back of the spoon.

TABLE OF CONTENTS

1

THE BASICS

2

RICH AND MOIST

3

FOAMY AND CREAMY

4

CRUNCHY AND SOFT

5

CAKES

6

CHIC AND PRECIOUS

7

PLAYFUL

RECIPE INDEX

THEMATIC INDEX

MILK CHOCOLATE

NUTS

WHITE CHOCOLATE

ACKNOWLEDGMENTS

A big thank you to Pierre Javelle for his sublime photos and his invaluable (and happy) cooperation! Thanks to Marabout, especially Rosemarie Di Domenico, who believed in us. Thanks to Audrey Génin for her meticulous preparation and her kindness. Thanks to Olivier Nikolcic for his pen. Thanks to Carl, whose little kindnesses were a treat.

Thanks to Pia Jonglez and Céline for the magnificent paintings from Ressource (Peinture Ressource, 2-4 du Maine avenue, Paris, 75015; www.ressource-peintures.com).

Thanks to Fernando at The Conran Shop (117 du Bac Street, Paris, 75007; www.conranshop.fr).

Thanks to Perrine Giry at 13 à Table (34 de Rivoli Street, Paris, 75004; www.13atable.com).

Thanks to Alexia at BHV (BHV Rivoli, 55 de la Verrerie Street, Paris Cedex 4, 75189; www.bhv.fr).